DELIVERANCE HANDBOOK

A GUIDE TO CASTING OUT DEMONS FOR TODAY'S CHRISTIAN

COMPANION TO *DELIVER US FROM EVIL* AND
A MANUAL OF DEMONOLOGY AND THE OCCULT

PASTOR KENT PHILPOTT

EVP

Earthen Vessel Publishing

Deliverance Handbook: A Guide to Casting Out Demons for Today's Christian (A Companion to *Deliver Us from Evil* and *A Manual of Demonology and the Occult*)

ISBN: 978-1-946794-24-6

Library of Congress Control Number: 2021931827
Cover design by Mary Keydash
Interior design by KLC Philpott

CONTENTS

PREFACE

This is a "handbook" on deliverance. The objective is to see deliverance ministry restored to the everyday life of the church, with the purpose being to help others learn how to do this work. It is hoped that church leaders/pastors will use this handbook to teach others how to conduct this vital ministry.

The second purpose for this book is to reach out to those who recognize their own need to be delivered from demonic forces.

Companions to this handbook are the re-publication of *A Manual of Demonology and the Occult* (San Rafael, CA: Earthen Vessel Publishing, 2020) and *Deliver Us From Evil: How Jesus Casts Out Demons Today*, 2014. These three books may be purchased as a "trilogy" or obtained individually.

I want to thank Karen Jankowski for preparing the 1977 edition for publication and Stephanie Adams for preparing that edition for this publication.

The forerunner to this handbook is *The Deliverance Book*, authored by Dr. R.L. Hymers, Jr. and me. It was published by Bible Voice of Los Angeles, California in 1977. It was written to slow the tide of people coming to us for deliverance ministry. We were literally being besieged in those days, the 1970's, so much so that we had a dozen teams trained to do the work.

Dr. Hymers, my old and good friend, granted me the right to rework that earlier book and update it to meet the circumstances in this era.

Kent Philpott, Pastor
Miller Avenue Baptist Church
Mill Valley, CA 94941

kentphilpott@comcast.net

milleravenuechurch.org and earthenversselmediacom

FOREWORD TO THE PRESENT EDITION

The Deliverance Book was originally published by Bible Voice in 1977. It has long since been out of print.

During the 1970s, there was an urgent need to deal with those coming to us in San Rafael, Marin County, California, to be delivered from demonic spirits.

My earliest view of the demonic had been formed by two degrees in psychology that led me to assume that the accounts of demons and the devil in the Bible were merely due to an inadequate understanding of mental illness. I recall being somewhat derisive of professors at Golden Gate Baptist Theological Seminary, then in Mill Valley, California, when they talked as though demons were real. I thought I knew better.

As a street preacher in San Francisco's Haight–Ashbury District, beginning in February of 1967, it did not take long before my concepts regarding the demonic were challenged. Once the actuality of the demonic became inescapably demonstrated, I decided to focus on the issue while a student for a ThM degree at the seminary in Mill Valley. The title of the thesis was *A Manual of Demonology and the Occult*. Zondervan Publishing House released it to the world in 1973, and my life changed. A new release of this in book form is available in mid-2021.

Desperate people began showing up in Marin County looking for me, since my book must have provided a modicum of hope. Mostly young adults, many having been immersed in the Beat and Hip cultures, had attracted demons to themselves through a variety of mechanisms. Some came by way of initiation ceremonies into various religious groups like the Society of Krishna Consciousness and Transcendental Meditation, others by involvement in Anton LaVey's Satanic Church, and still others via direct encounter with forms of the occult like astrology, mediums, fortune tellers, séances, and more.

That involvement might have been fun for a while, but then things had turned ugly and scary. With the publication of the manual, people began showing up at my door looking for relief. So then, for a decade at minimum, congregants who worked with me at the Church of the Open Door in San Rafael were dealing with what we then called "Deliverance Ministry." During the 1980s and onward, need for this ministry thankfully quieted down.

Fast forward to today, however, with contemporary occultism firmly entrenched in the culture, tagged a "Great Awokening," and the need arises again for this very biblical ministry of casting out of demons.

My recent effort at confronting the rise of interest in mystical and occult oriented practices is the short book entitled *Deliver Us from Evil: How Jesus Casts Out Demons Today*. Our Earthen Vessel Media published it in 2014, and it is available online as paperback or eBook.

Yes, a whole new generation has 'woken' up to all manner of spiritualities, not religions necessarily, but spiritually oriented practices. The Tarot, I Ching, astrology, the Ouija board, palm reading, séances, shamans galore, life coaches who use occult practices to help people direct their lives and learn to care for themselves above all things—this is the short list.

My efforts to avoid this kind of ministry failed. Much of this had to do with Tara Isabella Burton's book *Strange Rites*, which sparked a renewed awareness of the need to provide relief and healing for many who are now or will soon be looking for it and to completely revise *The Deliverance Book*, now entitled *Deliverance Handbook*.

Decades ago, the idea of demons and a devil was scoffed at, but not so much now. The world is alive with spirits—animal spirits and guide spirits to name a few— and strangely, sadly, many people are proud to have these spirits inside of them, since these spirits can provide empowering and even comfort. At least at first.

We therefore are presenting a trilogy of related books: *A Manual of Demonology and the Occult, Deliverance Handbook,* and *Deliver Us from Evil: How Jesus Casts Out Demons Today*. All of this is to help equip the Body of Christ to do the work of casting out of demons.

CHAPTER ONE

THE MINISTRY OF DELIVERANCE

As I walked into the Hare Krishna Temple in San Francisco, I was thinking of only one thing—how can I help some of these kids find Christ as their Savior?" It was the summer of 1967, and Kent Philpott had been doing evangelism in San Francisco for about six months. As a young Baptist preacher, he was unaware of the many pitfalls confronting a minister on the streets of this great metropolis at the height of the "Flower Children Era."

"I felt a demonic presence descend around me in a heavy cloud of gloom as I entered the temple," he relates. "I walked to the rear of the building, into the kitchen. Several of the devotees were busy preparing a meal. They knew who I was, and I felt anger in their eyes as I approached. I began to speak to one of them about salvation through Christ. The others grew increasingly angry. I realized that violence was about to break out, so I began to make a rather hurried exit.

"I walked back and out through the sanctuary of the temple. People were chanting and praying their mantras softly in the dusky shadows. As I got to the door, I stopped to talk for a minute to some of the kids who had followed me out from the kitchen.

"One of the boys was particularly angry with me for bringing the message of Christ into their temple. I looked into his eyes and sensed another set of eyes behind his, gazing out in white–hot rage.

"Then I remembered something one of my friends had told me a few weeks earlier at Golden Gate Baptist Seminary. We had talked for some time about demons and how to cast them out. This was the time, I thought, to put his theory into practice. If I had ever seen a demonized person, this was it!

"I pointed my finger at his face and said, 'Demon, I command you to come out in the name of Jesus Christ!' Before I could think, he lunged at me, grabbed me by the throat with both hands, and threw me hard against the wall. All thoughts of casting out demons disappeared instantly! I wasn't ready to die! I struggled out the door, and the two of us grappled across the sidewalk, as I tried to get away. I found myself pinned against the side of a parked car. He took hold of my shoulders with superhuman strength and threw me bodily in front of an oncoming car! Thank God, the car swerved just in time! I picked myself up from the pavement and dashed off down the street."

Thus, began the deliverance ministry of Kent Philpott! Over the next few months, he discovered how very little he actually knew about the demonic. Working exclusively with young drug addicts and perverts in the Haight–Ashbury district of San Francisco, he would be confronted again and again by the demonic. These experiences would cause him to dig into the Bible, to read Christian literature on the subject of deliverance, and to finally begin to formulate more mature ways of dealing with the devil's angels indwelling and troubling living human beings.[1]

DELIVERANCE VERSUS EXORCISM

Neither Jesus nor His apostles practiced "exorcism," that practice which was common in that era and had been many centuries among what are commonly referred to as pagans. Exorcise is an English word used to translate the Greek word *exorkizo* found only one time in the New Testament—Acts 19:13. The word describes a magical manipulation whereby spirits are supposedly cast out. In various English translations it is rendered "adjure" or "charge."

While Jesus and His followers did not practice the pagan rite of exorcism, they did practice Christian deliverance. The Greek word used to describe what Jesus and His followers did is *ekballo*. It means "to cast out." We see the "ek" and it is a Greek prefix meaning "out." Then we find "ball" as in baseball, something that is thrown. So, Jesus did not manipulate demons to leave through some kind of rite of exorcism. He commanded them to leave; He threw them out.

To restate: Exorcism (*exorkizo*) rituals or rites were never used by Jesus, Paul, or any of the apostles mentioned in the New Testament to drive out demons. The word is used of those who drive out demons by the use of rituals or magic formulas. There is no magic in Christian deliverance. There is nothing weird, strange, or cultic about it. Demons are simply "cast out" (*ekballo*) in the mighty name of Jesus! No crosses, no holy water, no incense, no dim lights, sanctified rooms, candles, special music need be employed. It is not necessary that speaking in tongues be employed. Just the name of Jesus! There is enough power in

---

1   The above was written by a person whose name I do not recall now. He was asked to re-write a book to be published by Zondervan Publishing House, in 1971. It was to be entitled *Two Brothers in Haight*, about me and David Hoyt, who had been a leading devotee at the temple. For reasons I cannot explain, the book was never published, but I have the original manuscript and stumbled upon the preceding passage.

that name alone to cast out every demon on earth!

In "Recommended Books" are a list of books I know will be of value to those interested in casting out demons. I suggest reading Richard Gallagher's book, *Demonic Foes*. He is an M.D., a psychiatrist, and Roman Catholic, having extensive experience with deliverance ministry. Though Roman Catholic exorcists employ complex "rites," such ministry can be effective.

A DISTINCTION

That said, the Roman Catholic Church's exorcism rites today are close to, but not the same as, the ministry recommended here. The principles are much the same, and should not be discounted. There has been a great deal of reform in the exorcism practices in the Roman Church over the centuries.

When I make a distinction between casting out of demons and "exorcism" I primarily have in mind shamanistic type "exorcisms" which do not depend upon the power of Jesus Christ of Nazareth but rely on magical and strange rites that are unbiblical. And aside from the Roman Catholic priests and deacons who conduct exorcisms, many Protestants and others refer to their ministries as "exorcism."

DEMONIZATION VERSUS POSSESSION

The English word "possession" is an interpretation of the Greek word *daimonizomia*. It means, literally, "demonize." The person seeking deliverance may indeed be "possessed," but this is an interpretation of the Greek word, not a literal translation of its meaning. Why is this important for you to know? The answer is, there are several words used to describe demonization, and the most common of these are:

POSSESSION – OBSESSION – OPPRESSION – DEPRESSION – COMPRESSION – INFESTATION

Having so many words and nuances to describe the activity or control of humans by demons is confusing. However, it is not so in the Bible. Not one of these words appears there! The Holy Spirit does not want to confuse us. He uses only ONE word, *daimonizomia* or "demonize."

One of the reasons this is important to understand is that the word "possession" may create false impressions. Demons, and there are only two other words used of demons in the New Testament—evil spirits and unclean spirits—except in rare instances have thorough or complete control of a person. It is not uncommon that I, and those with me, can see no obvious signs that demons are present at all.

The only concern we need have is discovering whether the person we are counseling or ministering to is demonized or not. Now, it is true that there are degrees of demonization. Again, to be demonized does not mean someone is totally controlled. There are very few people as demonized as the girl (based on the actual case of a young person) in The Exorcist. Most people are demonized to a much lesser extent than that.

Here are three statements of demonization that generally apply:

- A demon may have limited control or access to the one it is indwelling.
- A person may appear quite normal under most circumstances.
- Demons try to reduce a person mentally, spiritually, and physically, to gain more control.

Based only on my experience and that of others, I operate under the awareness that demons attempt to control a person to ever greater degrees. The steps are somewhat as follow:

- The person is slightly controlled.
- The person becomes controlled in certain areas of his or her life at first, but the number of these areas increases as he or she yields more and more of his or her life to the devil.
- The person becomes completely controlled, like the young girl in The Exorcist, or the Gerasene Demoniac (Mark 5:1–20).

Here is a brief summary of what has been presented so far: To be demonized is to be indwelt by an evil spirit. The degree of control that the spirit or spirits have on the individual may vary. It may be slight. It may be only in certain areas of the life, such as the sexual, the mental, the emotional, or certain physical areas. The person may be quite normal in every aspect but one or two. Or, the person's entire personality may be taken over by the demonic. The only people who usually become completely controlled are mediums or others who have deliberately devoted themselves to occult practices and/or actually give allegiance to Satan or his minions in some way, either currently or in the past. These individuals can move into a trance state and out of their own personalities, often without remembrance of their behavior or what happened during these occasions. Others who might become entirely dominated by demonization are those who have become mentally deranged in connection with it.

Most people are kept from this extreme degree of demonization by the natural protection of their will. The "will" (that part of our mind that says "yes" or "no") is placed about our personality like a fence or a wall to keep demonic influences out. (At least, this is an illustration that many who do this work attest to.) When that wall is broken down by sin, some demons may come in, especially in the area where the wall was broken. If a person regularly commits immoral sex, he or she removes the protective wall in that area of their personality and may become demonized sexually, no longer able to control themselves in that area, and are driven to the immoral by the demonic that is now controlling sexually. The protective "wall" in his or her mind has been broken down. Usually, the rest of that wall remains in place, protecting other areas of the personality. The entire wall can come down only in unusual and extreme cases. As previously stated, this usually happens only when a medium gives up his or her "will" completely to the demonic, or when a person becomes so insane, for one reason or another, that he or she is no longer in control of his or her "will."

It might be worth mentioning, and this statement comes from personal awareness of actual experience, that those who have been captured demonically into, for instance, habitual immoral sex, may become abnormally obsessed with preaching the importance of high biblical sexual ethics, judging others of sexual sin, all in utter contradiction to their own behavior.

Even more disturbing, some churches emphasize the emotional to the point that they actually jeopardize those who become caught up in the wildness of their services. I am acquainted with churches in which people reach up to shake hands with angels; sense the "brush of angel's wings" across their shoulders; and wait for the "breath of God" or "the sweet savor of the Lord to blow across their cheeks! These are counterfeit spiritual experiences. They are real experiences, but they are always demonic, and some people have actually become demonized in this way. God does not move in such a soulish, sensuous manner. That is why there is not one place in the Bible where such things take place!

THE GREAT MYSTERY

Before concluding this chapter, I think it is necessary to face the one great question that must come up for all of us who are aware of the presence of evil in our universe. Why?

Why did the Creator God allow the serpent to be in the Garden of Eden in the first place and then allow Eve and then Adam to be deceived? There is no record of even a warning given of an evil presence.

Why do we then have this ministry of casting out of demons? The answer is simple — because Satan is alive and well on planet earth and is seriously going about trying, really succeeding spectacularly, to destroy those whom God made in His image!

This, historically, is referred to as the problem of theodicy. No one throughout history has developed a satisfying answer. It is what it is. Will that work for you? Certainly not! We have to settle with the reality we face. One day, and that day will be in the presence of our Lord God, we will understand.

CHAPTER TWO

CAN A CHRISTIAN HAVE A DEMON?

I s it possible for a Christian to be demonized? This is one of the most controversial subjects in the Christian community today. People get into arguments, and churches have split over this question. Could anything be more incredible than that? It is always a sin to break fellowship or argue over such questions. Both sides are wrong for arguing and fighting over such trivial matters.

Both sides can point to their texts in the Bible as proof. Both can wax eloquent and verbose on the subject. But what really counts is ministry. Sometimes a person may be an excellent Christian for many years, but the demonized part of his or her life has never been dealt with. So of course, this person remains demonized.

Hal Lindsey has summed up my position:

> Semantics separating demon possession and demon influence seem important to some people. A person who is demon influenced is under the power of evil spirits, which may result in anything from mental torment to extreme abnormal behavior. Both believers and unbelievers can be subject to demon influence . . . a non–Christian can be totally controlled and manipulated by demonic power, but a Christian rarely has the same degree of complete subjugation. This is my position, also I've talked to many missionaries who have had to deal with these things personally, and I must say that it seems to be possible for a Christian to have a certain degree of demon possession. Whenever we deliberately turn from depending on the Holy Spirit to resist temptation, and then knowingly plot to commit sin, we open ourselves up for the possibility of Satanic attack and even control. [1]

I agree with Hal Lindsey, and I recall the days when he and Pat Matrisciana and I

---

1   Hal Lindsey with Carole C. Carlson, *Satan is Alive and Well on Planet Earth*, (Grand Rapids, MI: Zondervan Publishing House, 1972).

sat in my living room in Terra Linda, California, and worked on Hal's book, *Satan is Alive and Well on Planet Earth*.

A Christian can be demonized, at least in certain areas of his of her life. It is not understood how this is possible, but my experiences, along with those of many others, such as Don Basham, Derek Prince, and Dr. Richard Gallagher, reveal this quite clearly. I attest to this, because I have seen literally hundreds of Christians helped through deliverance ministry. Why refuse to give help to those who need it? And how can anyone be absolutely certain whether anyone is born again or not? As a long-time pastor, I have quite often been fooled as to a person's spiritual condition. In fact, some of the most "spiritual" of people later proved to be unconverted either by their leaving the faith or by a sudden experience of genuine conversion.

When followers of Jesus come to a point where they become aware of an evil presence, they will begin to look for relief. The presence will not be alluring but rather repulsing. This is the circumstance of believers who come looking for deliverance.

The question is not really one for theological debate. The real question is one of Christian ministry. Are we willing to offer real help through Jesus Christ to those who need it? That has to be the thought we hold central in our minds as we approach those who have experienced the ravages of the demonic in their lives.

Looking back now over the years, I have found few non-Christians seeking deliverance from demonic spirits. The vast majority of those who seek deliverance are confessing Christians who at some point in the past, almost always prior to their conversions, engaged in practices such as Ouija boards, psychic readings, astrology, Tarot, Reiki therapy, and other occultic forms. Or, perhaps, by means of drumming, dance, deep meditation, and more, have opened themselves up to the demonic. And sadly, I must report, that some have become invaded by evil spirits by means of so-called "spiritual" worship.

A BAG OF WORMS

This subject must be addressed now, no matter how reluctant I am to open a "bag of worms." But in light of what is going on in today's culture, it seems an imperative.

In 1988 and 1989, I attended the Church Growth Seminars, beginning and advanced sessions, at Fuller Theological Seminary in Pasadena, California. I had been in contact with C. Peter Wagner, a professor at the seminary, and spent hours with him and another professor, Charles Kraft, discussing the Jesus People Movement and deliverance ministry. One of the conference speakers was John Wimber, who spawned the Vineyard Church movement as a break away movement from Calvary Chapel churches.

Mr. Wimber's specialty was developing the worship environment, and chief was the use of lighting and especially music. Everything depended on the skill of the "worship leader" and the band. The goal was to prepare for the arrival of the Holy Spirit, which moved the worshippers into a state of spiritual "readiness" such that people were literally hearing what they thought was the voice of God, giving words of prophecy for themselves and others. The point is: Did such "worship" open the door to deception? Could something so foreign to the New Testament and the worship of the early believers open doors to something other than the Holy Spirit, all the while being very, very spiritual?

Though deliverance ministry could be enough of a focus, I have felt it necessary to reach out to those who have been spiritually and emotionally damaged by what is referred to as the New Apostolic Reformation, which began in 2000 through the efforts of C. Peter Wagner, now deceased, because I feel some sense of responsibility for it, however small.

After the conclusion of my work on this book, I am preparing a course of seminars to be available on-line to help those who have been damaged by this insidious movement. The series is based on six years of hosting a "Cult Recovery Support Group." It is not a simple thing to recover from the harm caused by over emphasis of some Christian aspects.

To illustrate: a friend of mine since high school days, and his wife, attended the Bethel Church in Redding, California, and were fully engaged in a number of different ministries there. On several occasions, I visited the church with my friends. Now however, a few years ago they confessed they had seen enough and had backed away. They are yet followers of Jesus but have decided to have their own devotional and worship at home, as they are afraid to attend another church in Redding.

If any reader would like to connect with the support group and view the sessions, please email me at kentphilpott@comcast.net.

CHAPTER THREE

GENERAL CONSIDERATIONS

GROUP DELIVERANCE?

Individual deliverance as opposed to group deliverance is the focus of this book and this chapter; however, I have prepared another chapter where I speak of group deliverance more extensively.

First, let us consider, what is wrong with group deliverance? For one thing, it usually prevents deliverance ministers from doing adequate personal "counseling" work. They cannot take the time necessary to counsel and work with the people to whom they are ministering. People are important as individuals, and a special ministry like deliverance is so tied up with the person's private, inner life, that it becomes nearly impossible to counsel and pray about these delicate issues in a room full of people.

That said, there may be a place for group deliverance ministry. Don Basham, from whom I have learned much of how to do deliverance in the first place, did successfully conduct group deliverance. In his book *Deliver us from Evil: A Pastor's Reluctant Encounters with the Powers of Darkness*, Pastor Basham describes such means of deliverance. He was essentially forced into group work, as there were times when it was necessary or it simply "broke out." Then, as time went on and other preachers and pastors heard of his work, group deliverance increased. The hope was that those who received deliverance were either members of churches or had friends who were. Thus, follow-up ministry would be available.

DELIVERANCE WITHIN A COMMUNITY OF BELIEVERS

Deliverance is best seen as part of the ministry of a biblical and gospel-oriented church or other community of followers of Jesus. It should not be thought of as a specialized ministry done by some people only. All pastors, elders, deacons, deaconesses, and other ministers should be equipped and ready to cast out demons.

17

This is particularly true in an age like our own, where there is so much extreme demonic activity going on throughout the culture.

Every single person who had demons cast out in the New Testament approached either Jesus or an apostle. Not once did Jesus or the apostles go to people and tell them they needed to have deliverance. That should teach us something about the ministry of deliverance. It is not to be evangelized. Great harm can be done if we overemphasize deliverance. Some of us have become so "demon–conscious" that we neglect prayer, personal evangelism, and the more important areas of Christian ministry. I have known churches becoming so involved with this particular ministry that they actually kept charts on each of their members, listing the demons that had been cast out, in what order, and what demons might yet remain! Such extremes are to be avoided.

Let us wait for people to come to us seeking deliverance. And they will come. That is how it was for Jesus and Paul as well. However, one thing that concerns me with the publication of this book and the other two which make up the trilogy of books on deliverance ministry and the occult is that it could trigger more awareness of the need for such ministry and therefore more requests for it than we can deal with.

ORDINARY VERSUS EXTRAORDINARY

People need to see that deliverance is an ordinary, common ministry that is not carried out by "specialists" in some dimly lit corner. It is not a sensational, kinky rite. It is a normal part of New Testament work!

For too long deliverance has been a "specialty" ministry, confined to a few "experts" who traveled around the country proclaiming themselves as "God's Man of the Hour." To repeat, this work should rather be a normal, everyday part of the life of biblically oriented churches.

Right motives are necessary to accomplish this goal of placing deliverance into the normal context of everyday church life. The goal should be twofold: We should desire to see God glorified; and we should seek to help brothers and sisters in their need for freedom and healing.

Deliverance should not be glamorized as a special ministry. In Luke 10:17–20, Luke reports:

> The seventy-two returned with joy and said, "Lord, even the demons submit to us in your name." He replied, "I saw Satan fall like lightning from heaven. I have given you authority to trample on snakes and scorpions, and to overcome all the power of the enemy; nothing will harm you. However, do not rejoice that the spirits submit to you, but rather rejoice that your names are recorded in heaven."

Jesus directly and clearly told the disciples that they should not get excited about casting out demons. They should see this as normal and as merely part of all the work that God had called them to do.

AUTHORITY VERSUS POWER

The power to do deliverance does not lie in the cleverness or personality of the one performing the ministry. This cannot be overemphasized. Some have the idea that only those with strong, powerful personalities, those with a good ability to communicate, or those with some other personal or spiritual quality or gifting will make good deliverance ministers.

The plain fact is that *any Christian* can do deliverance! Not that all Christians *should* do deliverance, but any can. Saying that not all should do it is because there are some who are not ready. They may be immature in their faith or personalities, or they may have significant sin in their lives. But it is nonetheless true that any born-again Christian, if they are not disqualified by some personal problem, can do this ministry.

You see, it is not our power that results in deliverance. It is the power of Jesus Christ that casts out demons. It is His power, not ours, that does the work.

Jesus has chosen to give us this work to do. He gives us the power, and He also gives us the authority. The Bible says, "When Jesus had called the Twelve together, he gave them power and authority to drive out all demons..." (Luke 9:1). Take careful note of the words, "power and authority." Jesus gives us *His* power and *His* authority to drive out demons.

PROTECTION VERSUS VULNERABILITY

Those who engage in deliverance ministry need to live a holy life. It's strange how the word "holy" has fallen into dispute today. It seems that some Christians would rather be anything other than holy. But holiness is what God has called us to, and it is holiness that we must have to be powerful for Christ in any area of Christian service. So, it is in deliverance.

Being holy, needing to be holy, is for many of us a scary concept. As followers of Jesus, we want to live godly lives, and if we should falter, we do have an advocate with the Father, Jesus Christ the righteous. Please carefully examine 1 John 1:8-2:2. Those engaging in deliverance ministry will remain humble and prayerful, remembering to confess their sins.

I confess that I was often tempted to crazy thinking prior to times of ministering deliverance. Weird and wicked thoughts would come to mind, which tended to intimidate me or even produce fear. To counteract these experiences, which again are common, we have the wonderful opportunity to come before Almighty God and bring our prayers of confession and ask for strength and courage.

Deliverance ministers need not fear being attacked by Satan. Notice I state, "fear being attacked," because we may well be attacked, but we need not fear it.

Scripture has this wonderful statement: "You, dear children, are from God and have overcome them, because the one who is in you is greater than he that is in the world" (1 John 4:4). These words of the Apostle John mean a lot to those who do the work of deliverance.

CHAPTER FOUR

JESUS
CASTS OUT DEMONS

The New Testament has at least six accounts of deliverance by Jesus, and others through His disciples. It is important that every deliverance minister be familiar with these accounts. Even if one has read them before, they should be read again and again for the new insight that the Holy Spirit can give regarding the ministry to which He is calling you.

1) THE MAN WITH THE UNCLEAN SPIRIT IN CAPERNAUM— MARK 1:21–28; LUKE 4:3–37

[21] And they went into Capernaum, and immediately on the Sabbath he entered the synagogue and was teaching. [22] And they were astonished at his teaching, for he taught them as one who had authority, and not as the scribes. [23] And immediately there was in their synagogue a man with an unclean spirit. And he cried out, [24] "What have you to do with us, Jesus of Nazareth? Have you come to destroy us? I know who you are—the Holy One of God." [25] But Jesus rebuked him, saying, "Be silent, and come out of him!" [26] And the unclean spirit, convulsing him and crying out with a loud voice, came out of him. [27] And they were all amazed, so that they questioned among themselves, saying, "What is this? A new teaching with authority! He commands even the unclean spirits, and they obey him." [28] And at once his fame spread everywhere throughout all the surrounding region of Galilee. (Mark 1:21–28)

Note that the unclean spirit recognized Jesus at once. Notice also the "us," referring to more than one, but only one spoke, and the demons were fearful. Fearful indeed, because these evil spirits recognized the power of Jesus. Several times, I have detected the fear of the demons when doing deliverance. Jesus commanded, "Be silent" and then ordered the spirits out of the man. And what followed is so very typical — the spirits convulsed him and cried out with a loud voice. Notice the "loud voice." The observers had never seen anything like it before.

A quick note here: During deliverance sessions one need not be frightened by the shrieks that come out of the person being delivered!

2) THE BLIND AND DUMB DEMONIAC—MATTHEW 12:22–29; MARK 3:22–27; LUKE 11:14–22

Here are both the Matthew and Mark passages.

> [22] Then a demon-oppressed man who was blind and mute was brought to him, and he healed him, so that the man spoke and saw. [23] And all the people were amazed, and said, "Can this be the Son of David?" [24] But when the Pharisees heard it, they said, "It is only by Beelzebul, the prince of demons, that this man casts out demons." (Matthew 12:22–24)

> [22] And the scribes who came down from Jerusalem were saying, "He is possessed by Beelzebul," and "by the prince of demons he casts out the demons." [23] And he called them to him and said to them in parables, "How can Satan cast out Satan? [24] If a kingdom is divided against itself, that kingdom cannot stand. [25] And if a house is divided against itself, that house will not be able to stand. [26] And if Satan has risen up against himself and is divided, he cannot stand, but is coming to an end. [27] But no one can enter a strong man's house and plunder his goods, unless he first binds the strong man. Then indeed he may plunder his house. (Mark 3:22-27)

Commenting on both the Matthew and Mark passages, we see the larger context. In Matthew, Jesus is casting demons out of a man described as being "demon-oppressed." The term in the Greek however is transliterated *daimonizomenos* (transliterated means replacing Greek letters with the equivalent English letters). The word is a participle, and the term means the man was indwelt with demons that apparently caused the man to be blind and unable to speak. The word "healed" is also in verse 22, and the Pharisees stated it was a case of demons being cast out and charged that Jesus must have accomplished this by the power of Beelzebul, a common term for Satan or the devil in that era.

In Mark's Gospel Jesus is defending His work and gives His opposers a parable, the point of which is that Satan does not cast out Satan. Within the parable is the truth that Satan had been overwhelmed, having been bound by a power greater that his own.

3) THE GERASENE DEMONIAC—MATTHEW 8:28–34; MARK 5:1–20; LUKE 8:26–39. HERE IS LUKE'S ACCOUNT.

> [26] Then they sailed to the country of the Gerasenes, which is opposite

Galilee. [27] When Jesus had stepped out on land, there met him a man from the city who had demons. For a long time he had worn no clothes, and he had not lived in a house but among the tombs. [28] When he saw Jesus, he cried out and fell down before him and said with a loud voice, "What have you to do with me, Jesus, Son of the Most High God? I beg you, do not torment me." [29] For he had commanded the unclean spirit to come out of the man. (For many a time it had seized him. He was kept under guard and bound with chains and shackles, but he would break the bonds and be driven by the demon into the desert.) [30] Jesus then asked him, "What is your name?" And he said, "Legion," for many demons had entered him. [31] And they begged him not to command them to depart into the abyss. [32] Now a large herd of pigs was feeding there on the hillside, and they begged him to let them enter these. So he gave them permission. [33] Then the demons came out of the man and entered the pigs, and the herd rushed down the steep bank into the lake and drowned.

[34] When the herdsmen saw what had happened, they fled and told it in the city and in the country. [35] Then people went out to see what had happened, and they came to Jesus and found the man from whom the demons had gone, sitting at the feet of Jesus, clothed and in his right mind, and they were afraid. [36] And those who had seen it told them how the demon-possessed man had been healed. [37] Then all the people of the surrounding country of the Gerasenes asked him to depart from them, for they were seized with great fear. So he got into the boat and returned. [38] The man from whom the demons had gone begged that he might be with him, but Jesus sent him away, saying, [39] "Return to your home, and declare how much God has done for you." And he went away, proclaiming throughout the whole city how much Jesus had done for him. (Luke 8:26-39)

In perhaps this most remarkable of all the New Testament's descriptions of Jesus casting out demons are found several crucial truths.

First, is that the demonized man was in severe bondage to the demons indwelling him. Rarely have I ever come across anything so radical, but such cases have been reported.

Second, the man fell at Jesus' feet and begged to be left alone. This I have personally witnessed.

Three, the demonized man had super-human strength. This is not unusual.

Four, we notice Jesus is speaking to only one demon but there were many more of them. It is characteristic that the most powerful of the demons will speak on behalf of the collection of them.

Five, Jesus asks for the name of the evil spirit and receives a reply. At times I have done this and at others I have not. It seems to have made little difference, but others with extensive experience in this area, more than my own, have found it of value. Some writers, such as Don Basham and Derek Prince, teach this is important.

Six, demons do not want to be cast out, as in being cast into hell; they prefer to be in flesh, even the flesh of animals. And this I have encountered as well. Demons will plead and beg not to be cast into hell, and this most of the time, showing the reality of an eternal hell. Let me say at this point, deliverance work confirms many issues that most of us Christians wonder about, even question. After some engagements with casting out of demons you will never question the reality of hell. It is real!

Seven, those who lived in the area and knew about the demonized man, instead of being happy for the wonderful miracle they had witnessed and the new life given to a hopeless individual, wanted Jesus to leave their area and never return.

Eight, the formerly demonized person wants to remain with Jesus. Those who are delivered of demons desperately do not want to leave Jesus and tend to be exceptional disciples. The man in this story became an evangelist.

Nine, the term "demon-possessed" in verse 36 should more properly be translated "demonized."

4) THE SYROPHOENICIAN WOMAN'S DAUGHTER—MATTHEW 15:21–28; MARK 7:24–30

> [21] And Jesus went away from there and withdrew to the district of Tyre and Sidon. [22] And behold, a Canaanite woman from that region came out and was crying, "Have mercy on me, O Lord, Son of David; my daughter is severely oppressed by a demon." [23] But he did not answer her a word. And his disciples came and begged him, saying, "Send her away, for she is crying out after us." [24] He answered, "I was sent only to the lost sheep of the house of Israel." [25] But she came and knelt before him, saying, "Lord, help me." [26] And he answered, "It is not right to take the children's bread and throw it to the dogs." [27] She said, "Yes, Lord, yet even the dogs eat the crumbs that fall from their masters' table." [28] Then Jesus answered her, "O woman, great is your faith! Be it done for you as you desire." And her daughter was healed instantly. (Matthew 15:22–28)

Jesus and disciples had traveled out of the main area of Israel and were near the eastern coast of the Mediterranean Sea where Gentiles or Canaanites lived. There was a great deal of racism between the two cultural/religious groups. In verse 22, we find in our text the term "oppressed by a demon" and again the word is a derivative that could be translated demonized.

It is not entirely possible to grasp the underlying give and take between Jesus and the Canaanite woman, but some commentators describe it as "light-hearted."

In verse 28 we find the word "healed," which is the proper term. We might expect to have there a word that corresponded to "cast out" or "expel," but "healed" is the word, and so it is that those who have demons cast out are indeed healed as well as delivered.

5) THE BOY WITH THE DEMON THAT FEIGNED EPILEPSY— MATTHEW 17:14–21; MARK 9:14–29; LUKE 9:37–43

[14] And when they came to the crowd, a man came up to him and, kneeling before him, [15] said, "Lord, have mercy on my son, for he has seizures and he suffers terribly. For often he falls into the fire, and often into the water. [16] And I brought him to your disciples, and they could not heal him." [17] And Jesus answered, "O faithless and twisted generation, how long am I to be with you? How long am I to bear with you? Bring him here to me." [18] And Jesus rebuked the demon, and it came out of him, and the boy was healed instantly. [19] Then the disciples came to Jesus privately and said, "Why could we not cast it out?" [20] He said to them, "Because of your little faith. For truly, I say to you, if you have faith like a grain of mustard seed, you will say to this mountain, 'Move from here to there,' and it will move, and nothing will be impossible for you." (Matthew 17:14–18)

A father with great concern for his son came to Jesus and reported that his son had seizures that resulted in near-death experiences such as falling into water or fire. The problem was that Jesus' disciples had been unable to help, so the father came directly to Jesus, who issued a rather serious lament after being made aware of the circumstances.

Jesus asked the father to bring his son to Him, and he did. Jesus "rebuked" the demon, which came out of him, with the resulting report that the boy was "healed."

The disciples, obviously quite stunned by it all, wanted to know why they had been ineffective. Jesus' response may well strike us as problematic. Rather than a lack of suitable training, the cause of the failure, Jesus stated, had to do with a lack of faith.

This account has perplexed and sometimes caused me to wonder if I really had enough faith to do deliverance ministry; and to be honest about it, there were times when I saw no results and would wonder if the problem was my insufficient faith. At this point, I have no clear answer, but it does not dissuade me from continuing in this work. Despite having engaged in this ministry for several decades, questions remain.

6) THE WOMAN WITH A SPIRIT OF INFIRMITY—LUKE 13:10–17

[10] Now he was teaching in one of the synagogues on the Sabbath. [11] And behold, there was a woman who had had a disabling spirit for eighteen years. She was bent over and could not fully straighten herself. [12] When Jesus saw her, he called her over and said to her, "Woman, you are freed from your disability." [13] And he laid his hands on her, and immediately she was made straight, and she glorified God. [14] But the ruler of the synagogue, indignant because Jesus had healed on the Sabbath, said to the people, "There are six days in which work ought to be done. Come on those days and be healed, and not on the Sabbath day." [15] Then the Lord answered him, "You hypocrites! Does not each of you on the Sabbath untie his ox or his donkey from the manger and lead it away to water it? [16] And ought not this woman, a daughter of Abraham whom Satan bound for eighteen years, be loosed from this bond on the Sabbath day?" ((Luke 13:10–16)

"Disability" found in verses 11 and 12 may be more accurately translated "infirmity." Those around her assumed she was suffering from a physical ailment that resulted in her being unable to stand up straight.

The day of the healing was a Sabbath, and the location was a synagogue. The healing was considered "work," which was not allowed on a Sabbath. Yes, there was something terribly amiss here, and Jesus unloads on the leaders. He points out something they all knew. Of course, if an animal was in danger or simply thirsty, having gotten that way on a Sabbath Day, it would certainly be rescued or led to water. And here was not an animal but an actual person!

The reason this passage is notable in the context of our study here is that Jesus says, "whom Satan bound for eighteen years." The problem was not so much a physical one; it was spiritually satanic. Only Jesus would have known this.

And this changes everything. What appeared to be a healing was much more—it was a casting out of demons, here referred to as being loosed from Satan's bond.

7) FOLLOWING NOW ARE OTHER INSTANCES IN THE NEW TESTAMENT WHERE IT IS MENTIONED THAT JESUS CAST DEMONS OUT OF PEOPLE.

MATTHEW 4:23–24

[23] And he went throughout all Galilee, teaching in their synagogues and proclaiming the gospel of the kingdom and healing every disease and every affliction among the people. [24] So his fame spread throughout all Syria, and they brought him all the sick, those afflicted with various diseases and pains, those oppressed by demons, those having seizures, and paralytics, and he healed them.

We note that Matthew makes a distinction between those who were sick, afflicted with various diseases and pains, and those who were oppressed by demons. Again, "oppressed" comes from the word meaning demonized.

MATTHEW 8:14-16

[14] And when Jesus entered Peter's house, he saw his mother-in-law lying sick with a fever. [15] He touched her hand, and the fever left her, and she rose and began to serve him. [16] That evening they brought to him many who were oppressed by demons, and he cast out the spirits with a word and healed all who were sick.

Observe the difference, once again, between healing and casting out of demons. Of interest, is that Jesus cast out demons "with a word." This frankly has baffled me. Never in my experience have I seen deliverance from evil spirits done with a single word. Mostly, it is a profusion of words and more words.

MARK 1:32–34

[32] That evening at sundown they brought to him all who were sick or oppressed by demons. [33] And the whole city was gathered together at the door. [34] And he healed many who were sick with various diseases, and cast out many demons. And he would not permit the demons to speak, because they knew him.

Again a difference is evident, a distinction between the healing of physical illnesses and the casting out of demons. Curiously, here is something rather new: Jesus does not permit the demons to speak. Perhaps it is that Jesus, in this early period of His ministry, did not want to have His work dominated by healings and casting out of demons. This is merely a guess, as the text does not directly reveal a clear answer. Another guess is that, since the demons "knew him," Jesus might not have wanted them to announce who He was at this early stage. The two ideas are compatible.

In Luke 4:41 we find the same account as Mark 1:32–34.

LUKE 8:1-2

[1] Soon afterward he went on through cities and villages, proclaiming and bringing the good news of the kingdom of God. And the twelve were with him, [2] and also some women who had been healed of evil spirits and infirmities: Mary, called Magdalene, from whom seven demons had gone out, [3] and Joanna, the wife of Chuza, Herod's household manager, and Susanna, and many others, who provided for them out of their means.

In Jesus' evangelistic ministry, accompanied by the Twelve, some women who were also present had not only been healed of physical ailments but also had demons cast out. And here we meet Mary Magdalene, from whom seven demons had been cast out.

It is abundantly clear that the casting out of demons was a routine aspect of Jesus' ministry.

CHAPTER FIVE

THE DISCIPLES
CAST OUT DEMONS

THEIR MINISTRY PRIOR TO THE ASCENSION

MARK 6:7–13 — JESUS SENDS OUT THE TWELVE

[7] And he called the twelve and began to send them out two by two, and gave them authority over the unclean spirits. [8] He charged them to take nothing for their journey except a staff—no bread, no bag, no money in their belts—[9] but to wear sandals and not put on two tunics. [10] And he said to them, "Whenever you enter a house, stay there until you depart from there. [11] And if any place will not receive you and they will not listen to you, when you leave, shake off the dust that is on your feet as a testimony against them." [12] So they went out and proclaimed that people should repent. [13] And they cast out many demons and anointed with oil many who were sick and healed them.

Jesus sent out the Twelve Apostles and gave them authority over evil spirits. And in the process, Mark tells us that they did indeed cast out "many demons." Also, others who were sick were healed, and the point here is the difference. Unclean spirits were not cast out of those who needed healing.

LUKE 10:17–20 — THE RETURN OF THE SEVENTY-TWO

[17] The seventy-two returned with joy, saying, "Lord, even the demons are subject to us in your name!" [18] And he said to them, "I saw Satan fall like lightning from heaven. [19] Behold, I have given you authority to tread on serpents and scorpions, and over all the power of the enemy, and nothing shall hurt you. [20] Nevertheless, do not rejoice in this, that the spirits are subject to you, but rejoice that your names are written in heaven."

At another point in time, following the sending out of the Twelve, seventy-two

29

others were also sent out by Jesus, apparently two by two. Upon their return, with joy they reported that the demons were subject to them, meaning the unclean spirits had to obey them, because the demons were "subject" to them due to Jesus' "name."

It is highly important that we understand what it means that the demons were "subject to us in your name." First, it is not a magical event—no oaths, curses, etc., were uttered containing the name of Jesus. Then "name" has to do with who Jesus is—His person, His authority, His power. And note that these two events, the sending out of the Twelve and the seventy-two came before Jesus' crucifixion, resurrection, and ascension. Frankly, this is difficult to explain, but that it happened as it says in Luke's Gospel is believable. Why else would Luke have included the episode?

It is also crucial for all who engage in deliverance work to see that Jesus is careful that His followers not be too elated that demonic spirits were subject to them. I recall making that same error early on. Wow, demons even, had to come out of a person because of my ministry! Jesus warned the seventy-two, and thus all followers of Jesus down through the ages, not to "rejoice" that the spirits are subject to us, but more importantly, that our names are recorded in heaven, meaning, that we have a salvation that can never be revoked.

THEIR MINISTRY FOLLOWING THE ASCENSION

ACTS 5:12–16 MANY SIGNS AND WONDERS DONE

> [12] Now many signs and wonders were regularly done among the people by the hands of the apostles. And they were all together in Solomon's Portico. [13] None of the rest dared join them, but the people held them in high esteem. [14] And more than ever believers were added to the Lord, multitudes of both men and women, [15] so that they even carried out the sick into the streets and laid them on cots and mats, that as Peter came by at least his shadow might fall on some of them. [16] The people also gathered from the towns around Jerusalem, bringing the sick and those afflicted with unclean spirits, and they were all healed.

As the days passed following Pentecost Sunday in Jerusalem, the believers in Jesus continued to cast out unclean spirits. This work became normative. The history of the church through the centuries, however, reveals that there were periods when this work was evident, but also, and even more clearly, that the casting out of demons was neglected or changed in ways that essentially diminished or perverted this highly important ministry.

The same can be said in this twenty-first century. Decades ago, there were many "deliverance ministries," but now there are few. Why this is so is not clear, with likely an assortment of explanations, but today in our current cultural climate with the explosion of what is often termed "contemporary occultism," more and more people are being exposed to demonic spirits and are becoming demonized. May it be that our Lord will raise up a cadre of Christians who will be willing to step out to accomplish this ministry.

ACTS 8:4–8 PHILIP PROCLAIMS CHRIST IN SAMARIA

[4] Now those who were scattered went about preaching the word. [5] Philip went down to the city of Samaria and proclaimed to them the Christ. [6] And the crowds with one accord paid attention to what was being said by Philip, when they heard him and saw the signs that he did. [7] For unclean spirits, crying out with a loud voice, came out of many who had them, and many who were paralyzed or lame were healed. [8] So there was much joy in that city.

The ministry of Philip (not the Apostle Philip, but the deacon Philip of Acts 6:1–5), travelled to Samaria, a place that was not completely safe for a Jew. Philip preached Jesus there and drew the attention of the locals because of "signs" that he did, among which, besides healings, was the casting out of unclean spirits. Notice that the demons came out "crying with a loud voice." Further we note that Luke writes that this was apparent in "many," implying not all.

This point is important, because it is the same experience for those who do deliverance ministry today. The screaming of the demons as they are cast out is usual. On two separate occasions our team of deliverance ministers caught the attention of the police—due to loud screams issuing from people when demons were coming out. I must confess that it took a rather long while before I was not startled and upset by the loud wailings.

PAUL ACTS 16:16–19

[16] As we were going to the place of prayer, we were met by a slave girl who had a spirit of divination and brought her owners much gain by fortune-telling. [17] She followed Paul and us, crying out, "These men are servants of the Most High God, who proclaim to you the way of salvation." [18] And this she kept doing for many days. Paul, having become greatly annoyed, turned and said to the spirit, "I command you in the name of Jesus Christ to come out of her." And it came out that very hour. [19] But when her owners saw that their hope of gain was gone, they seized Paul and Silas and dragged them into the marketplace before the rulers.

Deliverance ministry can land the minister in trouble, as it happened to Paul and company. Here, a slave girl played the role of a medium or psychic by doing divination, attracting many clients and making her owners wealthy. It isn't clear whether she sought out Paul and Silas or happened to be there. Also unclear is whether she had previously become a believer, became a believer under their influence, or knew by virtue of her demonic psychic ability that Paul and company were actual servants of God.

In any case, Paul had enough of the disturbance she created and commanded her empowering demon to come out.

We note again the phrase, "the name of Jesus Christ." And once again, we note that Paul was not using a magical formula on the slave girl. No, Paul wanted all to know, especially the demon, that it was Jesus and not he himself who was casting out the demon.

What this meant for Paul and his associates was likely not an anticipated event — dragged in front of the "rulers." Our point here is that deliverance ministry can be dicey, dangerous even, and may produce some real trouble, just as likely in this day as that.

PAUL ACTS 19:11–20 THE SONS OF SCEVA

[11] And God was doing extraordinary miracles by the hands of Paul, [12] so that even handkerchiefs or aprons that had touched his skin were carried away to the sick, and their diseases left them and the evil spirits came out of them. [13] Then some of the itinerant Jewish exorcists undertook to invoke the name of the Lord Jesus over those who had evil spirits, saying, "I adjure you by the Jesus whom Paul proclaims." [14] Seven sons of a Jewish high priest named Sceva were doing this. [15] But the evil spirit answered them, "Jesus I know, and Paul I recognize, but who are you?" [16] And the man in whom was the evil spirit leaped on them, mastered all of them and overpowered them, so that they fled out of that house naked and wounded. [17] And this became known to all the residents of Ephesus, both Jews and Greeks. And fear fell upon them all, and the name of the Lord Jesus was extolled. [18] Also many of those who were now believers came, confessing and divulging their practices. [19] And a number of those who had practiced magic arts brought their books together and burned them in the sight of all. And they counted the value of them and found it came to fifty thousand pieces of silver. [20] So the word of the Lord continued to increase and prevail mightily.

There is so much here! Paul was now in Ephesus, and there were miracles galore.

Healings by means that puzzle most Christians, as we do not see it elsewhere, and evil spirits coming out of people. The how or method of this casting out is not given in the text.

In Ephesus, some Jewish itinerant exorcists were also operating. They were the "seven sons of Sceva." Paul and company would have known of such operations, as it was a familiar practice in that day and for centuries before and after, not to mention still today.

Apparently, they had witnessed Paul uttering the name of Jesus and casting out demons, prompting the seven sons to copy him. "I adjure you by the Jesus whom Paul proclaims," they said to those who came to them for help.

We note the word "adjure." The pagan exorcists saw this as a powerful magical formula as they witnessed the success of the Christian ministry. The use of the term adjure reveals this. It was not a word Paul and his companions used.

The problem is that the phrase in the mouth of the exorcists did nothing more that stir up the demons in people that then proceeded to mock the seven sons of Sceva. The result was a most incredible embarrassment to the seven.

Despite it all, this proved to be an unusual blessing. Word of what happened to the exorcists spread quickly and broadly, and the result was large numbers of people brought there "books" together and made a big bonfire of them. What might have been a disaster turned out to be something whereby the "Word of the Lord continued to increase and prevail mightily."

CHAPTER SIX

HOW DEMONIZATION OCCURS

In speaking of avenues to demonization, I am describing ways in which a person becomes vulnerable to invasion by demons. The material for this chapter has come primarily from basic biblical principles but has also grown out of research and personal experiences in deliverance.

There are four primary ways by which people open themselves to invasion by demons. There is some overlapping of these four avenues, and of course, there are bound to be gaps in my knowledge. These four basic categories do, however, provide useful tools in determining whether deliverance is needed in an individual's life.

THE OCCULT

The occult is unquestionably the main avenue through which people become demonized. The following passages from the Bible clearly reveal that the occult is an abomination to God, a stench in his nostrils: Deuteronomy 18:10–12; 4:19; Leviticus 19:26,31; 20:6,27, 2 Kings 23:5; Galatians 5:20, and Revelation 21:8. One of the most important passages showing that God hates the occult is Deuteronomy 18:9–12:

> [9] "When you come into the land that the LORD your God is giving you, you shall not learn to follow the abominable practices of those nations. [10] There shall not be found among you anyone who burns his son or his daughter as an offering, anyone who practices divination or tells fortunes or interprets omens, or a sorcerer [11] or a charmer or a medium or a necromancer or one who inquires of the dead, [12] for whoever does these things is an abomination to the LORD. And because of these abominations the LORD your God is driving them out before you. [13] You shall be blameless before the LORD your God, [14] for these nations, which you are about to dispossess, listen to fortune-tellers and to diviners. But as for you, the LORD your God has not allowed you to do this.

34

Witchcraft, fortune telling (divination), spiritism (calling back the dead), and all omens and occult practices are detestable to God. That is a very strong word, detestable. God detests, despises, and hates such practices according to the Word of God. And Galatians 5:20 and Revelation 21:8 communicate the same under the New Covenant. The passage in Revelation is particularly graphic:

> [8] But as for the cowardly, the faithless, the detestable, as for murderers, the sexually immoral, sorcerers, idolaters, and all liars, their portion will be in the lake that burns with fire and sulfur, which is the second death."

It is obviously clear that God detests the occult. One of the main reasons this is true is because God knows that demons can easily take advantage of those who practice such things. That is because those who engage in occult practices have purposely set aside trust, honor, and obedience to the God of Creation. Their allegiance has been placed elsewhere. Practicing or engaging in any form of the occult is without question the main way in which people become demonized.

A partial listing of occult practices includes three major categories: (1) Fortune telling; (2) Magic; (3) Spiritism.

1. Fortune telling
    a.   Astrology
    b.   Palm reading
    c.   Tarot
    d.   I Ching
    e.   Ouija board
    f.   Fortune Teller
    g.   Tea Leaf Readings

2. Magic
    a.   Witchcraft
    b.   Satan worship
    c.   Curses and spells
    d.   Love magic and hate magic
    e.   Use of crystals for healing and other purposes

3. Spiritism
    a.   Seances
    b.   Mediumship
    c.   Clairvoyance
    d.   Hypnotherapy
    e.   Mental Telepathy
    f.   Clairaudience
    g.   Automatic Writing

h.   Trance States
i.   Reiki
j.   Astral Projection — out of body experiences.
k.   Shamanistic Practices
l.   The Soul Journey
m.   Use of the Enneagram
n.   The worship in the Native American Churches

It is important to realize that all of the above fall into the category of the occult according to the Bible. One is just as bad as another. It is every bit as harmful to consult the Ouija board as it is to worship Satan or practice black magic. It is just as demonic to read tea leaves or have one's palm read as it is to call the 'souls' of the dead back in a séance. All are occultic. All pave the way to the one practicing them to become demonized. All are detestable in the sight of Almighty God and this for our own good.

I have made a point of saying that one part of the occult is just as bad as another for a good reason. Many people think that palm reading, I Ching, or a Ouija board are just harmless fun and that reading tea leaves is child's play. These do not realize that they are playing with fire, and that often the fire burns deeply, leaving psychological and spiritual scars that last for years.

THE PASSIVE STATE OF MIND — ALTERED STATE OF CONSCIOUSNESS, SHAMANISTIC STATE OF MIND, TRANCE STATE, DEEP MEDITATION

The second avenue in which a person may become demonized is through going into a passive state of mind. There are two main ways that the passive state of mind occurs: (1) through trances, when the mind is neutral, open, and vulnerable; (2) through induced states or voluntary letting go, usually through drugs like magic mushrooms and psilocybin, chanting, drumming, the rattle, ganga, spiritualized forms of yoga, Transcendental Meditation, and much more.

The mind, as stated before, has a protective wall about it, provided by the will — this is our ability to say "no" to what is wrong and "yes" to what is right. Entering into a passive state of mind opens the door allowing the demonic to invade a person's psyche; the person may become partially or even completely controlled by the demonic. The passive state of mind that comes through certain types of meditation, is very dangerous in this respect, especially now when deep meditative practices are popular. The protective guard of the will comes down and the demonic may enter.

Deep forms of meditation are probably the most dangerous occult practice in America today, because it appears so harmless. It just seems like the practitioner is relaxing. But the type of relaxation practiced brings the protective barrier down and actually invites the demonic in! Scores of people have become demonized in this manner.

LSD, psilocybin, and other hallucinogens remove the protective barrier of the will, as does peyote and mescaline. (Peyote is commonly used in the Native American Churches.) There are also questions about the use of marijuana. These drugs remove the wall of the will and allow the demonic to enter. Many who have taken LSD or other mind-expanding substances have been demonized in this way.

It is appropriate to mention the Esalen Institute in Big Sur, California, at this point. What goes under the rubric of relaxation and mind expansion is really nothing more than an opening to the spirit world. Very dangerous.

The passive state of mind can come through trances induced in over-the-top Christian worship as well. Some hyper–Pentecostal groups work their worshippers up to a frenzy foreign to what we find in the New Testament. Those in the services may enter a passive state of mind and become demonized. Some people even think that they have been filled with the Holy Spirit, when it was actually a demon that entered them. Many today ask why some hyper–pentecostal groups react so violently to sound teaching on demonization, especially concerning the fact that church members may become demonized. A passive state of mind is extremely dangerous, whether it be in a church sanctuary, at a drumming group, a cleansing in a sweat lodge, or focusing for an hour on breathing techniques.

Hypnotism has come into vogue again, too, and here is a direct and willful attempt to move into a passive state of mind.

EXCESSIVE SIN

Another avenue through which the demonic may enter a person is through excessive sin. The protective wall of the will is removed, and people become vulnerable to Satan when, through rebellion and rejection of God and His Word, they commit themselves to sin or to a sinful lifestyle.

All Christians sin. That much is quite clear in the Bible. We are told, in the first chapter of 1 John, that if we say we have not sinned we make Him a liar and the truth is not in us. Clearly, therefore, Christians sin. First John, chapter 2, tells us that we have an advocate, Jesus Christ. We are told to confess our sins as they come into our lives, in order to remain in good fellowship with the Father.

However, when someone, Christian or not, deliberately rejects the prompting of the Holy Spirit and deliberately rebels against the Word of God, the Ten Commandments, and the Sermon on the Mount, that person opens himself or herself to the possibility of becoming demonized, particularly when the sin is excessive, as when the people "give themselves up" to the sin. Sadly, some commit themselves to sexual sins, to alcohol, to drugs, to the occult, and to many other areas of sin. They literally give over the center of their lives to wrongful and dangerous behavior. Such persons will certainly open themselves up to invasion by the demonic. The following verse describes what has been called the opening of oneself to a reprobate mind.

ROMANS 1:21–28

[21] For although they knew God, they did not honor him as God or give thanks to him, but they became futile in their thinking, and their foolish hearts were darkened. [22] Claiming to be wise, they became fools, [23] and exchanged the glory of the immortal God for images resembling mortal man and birds and animals and creeping things.

[24] Therefore God gave them up in the lusts of their hearts to impurity, to the dishonoring of their bodies among themselves, [25] because they exchanged the truth about God for a lie and worshiped and served the creature rather than the Creator, who is blessed forever! Amen.

[26] For this reason God gave them up to dishonorable passions. For their women exchanged natural relations for those that are contrary to nature; [27] and the men likewise gave up natural relations with women and were consumed with passion for one another, men committing shameless acts with men and receiving in themselves the due penalty for their error.

[28] And since they did not see fit to acknowledge God, God gave them up to a debased mind to do what ought not to be done.

Whatever else this dreadful passage may mean, this much is certain: giving oneself up to sin paves the way for the demonic to enter in.

Haven't you known people who ruined their minds to such an extent that they just could not make a real commitment to Christ? They have literally ruined their minds through sin. Despite all this, they may be freed from sin and experience deliverance. We do not give up on those caught in extreme rebellion. These people may be pleasantly surprised. Sometimes the very worst of people come around and become excellent Christians.

TRAUMATIC EXPERIENCES

Traumatic experiences may also pave the way for the demonic to come into a person's life. By "traumatic" is meant a potent emotional experience that so changes a person's psyche that the mental barrier comes down and the demonic comes in.

Fear is very often the emotion that produces this removal of the mental pro-tective barrier. An extremely traumatic fear experience, particularly in child-hood, can produce not only neurotic or psychotic experiences, but even demonic behavior in later years.

This type of demonization is rarer than the first three. But it is common enough that I felt it should be listed.

A famous example of the demonic entering through trauma is in the motion picture, *Three Faces of Eve*. This movie is based on the true story of a woman who became demonized as a child when her mother held her over a coffin and forced her to kiss the face of her dead grandmother. The child became demon-ized through the trauma of that moment, which caused the barriers of her mind to come down and the demonic to come in.

A sudden death of a loved one may produce so much hatred toward God on the part of a child that the child is vulnerable to the demonic. A child abandoned by his parents may become so thoroughly traumatized that the demonic comes in. Strong hatred of parents can produce demonization. A sexually abused child may be so scarred that it triggers a demonic event.

Now someone may feel that this "is not fair." Point taken; indeed, it does not seem fair that a child should suffer for the sins of parents or other adults. But we cannot blame God either. The Creator God allows humans to have free will and to do as they please. When dramatic, tragic events happen wherein children are heavily emotionally impacted, it may well produce long term emotional and spiritual disturbances.

Summing Up

In counseling with someone who may be demonized, which is part of the work necessary prior to actual sessions of casting demons out, it is essential to engage in discussions regarding past history. That is why it is necessary to have at least one preliminary session in which you can learn something of a person's back-ground. (More will be said of this later.) It is vital to discover if the person has opened any of the aforementioned avenues through which demonization can come. Check whether they have engaged in any occult practices; whether they have ever entered a passive state of mind or have been involved in excessive sin. If none of these are in the background, yet you suspect that the person may be demonized, probe back into his or her past to see if there has been a heavily traumatic experience that could have opened the way for demonization.

Dr. Billy Graham best summed up the way people become demonized through Transcendental Meditation when he said: "People practicing TM wipe the slates of their minds clean, in effect, in an effort to establish a state of serenity and well–being. But in doing so, many are liable to create a vacuum in their minds. What goes into that empty space is the hidden danger of TM. It can be an invasion of satanic influences (demons) which will have an adverse effect on their lives."

(Note here: TM is no longer widely practiced and has virtually fallen out of public view. However, Dr. Graham's council or warning is yet relevant, due to the common practices that bring people into passive states of mind.)

Anything that "wipes the slate of the mind clean" and "creates a vacuum" in the mind by pulling down the barriers of the will can open a person to demonization.

CHAPTER SEVEN

HOW TO KNOW IF DELIVERANCE IS NEEDED

The material is this chapter has similarities to chapter six but is different enough to be included here.

DISCERNMENT

One of the most important ways to know if a person needs deliverance is through the gift of "distinguishing between spirits," also known as the gift of discernment. This is the charismatic gift mentioned in 1 Corinthians 12:10: "the ability to distinguish between spirits." This gift is really a rather simple one. Christians need to be able to tell the difference between what is true and false, who is lost and who is saved, and who is demonized and who is not. This gift helps us in all these areas.

Some years ago, I was preaching in a church near San Francisco. I looked up and saw a woman coming into the service late. The thought struck me, "That woman is demonized." Then I thought, "No, I don't even know her. I shouldn't think that!" But each time I looked at the woman the thought returned, "She's demonized." Later, at the request of members of her family, I was invited to the woman's house and spent some time talking to her. Sure enough, following counsel and prayer, it became evident that she was demonized!

This was the first time I realized just how the gift of discernment may operate. It is a gift from the Holy Spirit, so, of course, it defies human explanation. We may expect that the Holy Spirit will show us who needs deliverance. It is reasonable to ask God to give such discernment. It is reasonable to believe that God is able and willing to give His children every gift necessary to do His work.

OCCULT INVOLVEMENT

When someone has had clear involvement with the occult, we should suspect that the demonic may be present, since involvement with occult practices potentially puts a person in contact with demons. Indeed, everyone who has been involved with the occult might be a candidate for deliverance. It is better to err by being too careful than to be careless, which may result in people remaining demonized. Reading occult books may not produce demonization. But being steeped in this kind of literature may produce a mindset that makes one prone to being drawn into the demonic. It is spiritually unhealthy to fill one's mind with books on the occult. It may result in a person becoming morbidly fascinated with the demonic. It then becomes easier for Satan to tempt such a person to get more deeply involved. So, while the reading of occult literature itself may not open one to being demonized, it may pave the way to more serious involvement. It is sort of the "pornography" of the spirit world.

The occult operates much like sex in the way it tempts. Sexual sins are usually progressive in the way they involve the one indulging in them. A person starts out reading soft–core pornography; he or she soon progresses to hard–core material, then to "X" rated movies, then . . .. Well, anything can follow, and it often does. In like fashion, people also get involved progressively in the occult. They start out with astrology and progress to witchcraft. That is the way of all sin— start small and grow, grow, grow.

EXCESSIVE FEAR

Everyone is afraid from time to time. But excessive and prolonged fear is different. Sometimes such fear is called a neurosis, such as claustrophobia (fear of confined spaces), acrophobia (fear of heights), necrophobia (fear of death or dead things), and many others, and such fear has been known to trigger a demonic event.

There are different types of fear:

1.   Normal fear – produced by danger.
2.   Neurotic fear – produced by something in the person's past that he or she recalls, and so re–experiences the fear.
3.   Demonic fear – like neurotic fear but tending to bring the person into bondage of Satan. It is more than simple neurotic fear; it is fear that causes the person to commit to sinful practices.

Demonic fear must be broken before the person can experience freedom and joy in that area of his or her life.

Then too, demonic fear often interrupts a person's life. It tends to disrupt sleep, work, and normal life. Perhaps a person must sleep with a night light on, because a demon attaching itself to the fear of darkness (nyctophobia) keeps him or her in constant fear. When these people go through deliverance, they may well experience freedom from old fears that have plagued them for years.

The Bible states, "For God hath not given us the spirit of fear; but of power, and of love, and of a sound mind" (2 Timothy 1:7, KJV). The power of God's Spirit is fully capable of delivering us from all demonic fears as we yield our lives to Him.

Unusual Reaction to Christ and the Bible

Often those who are demonized react strangely to the message of Christ and the Bible. Sometimes even the name of Jesus can bring an unusual reaction. I recall a time when I encountered a young man who jumped up from the floor each time the name "Jesus" was said. Every time I said "Jesus" the young man leaped up uncontrollably! At other times, people will react violently to Bible messages, sermons, or prayers. Sometimes they will verbally or physically try to hinder preachers or Bible teachers. They may make a commotion in the Bible study or sermon. They seem unable to control themselves and will cough and squirm, especially at crucial moments, when central truths of the Christian message are being pressed home. Or they may go to sleep in such a way as to disturb those around them.

Fear of prayer, worship, or praise may be another indication of demonization. When the demonized child in The Omen reacted violently about being taken into a church, the author of the screenplay was reflecting something that is often true of the demonized. It is not uncommon for people to become unusually disturbed when the Blood of Christ, the Resurrection, the Second Coming, or the power of the Holy Spirit are mentioned.

In one circumstance, a person was not able to enter a church building. She would say to her husband, "There are just too many people in there." It didn't matter how few people were there; she could not go in. The woman remained demonized for years, and when confronted with the obvious fact, she replied in great outbursts of violent anger that "a Christian cannot possibly be demonized!"

Those of us who do deliverance will not be surprised or intimidated by such events.

Demonic Torments

Over the years, certain activities have occurred to people that were strange, weird, and unusual. Is it possible some of these had a demonic origin? Demons jumping on a bed, as portrayed in The Exorcist, or voices being heard when no one was present, physical attacks that defy understanding, such as being injured in strange ways with marks, scratches, and bruises appearing on arms, legs, or face. People may even experience sexual intercourse with an incubus or succubus (sexual demon). One instance comes to mind, that of a young married woman who was led out of her home night after night and driven to have sex with the first person she met. If she stayed in bed, an incubus, a demon disguised as a male, would have sex with her. (I do understand that some of these descriptions may cause some to question my veracity or even mental stability, but these are actual events.)

Demonic torments are very real. Many people are experiencing them in our society. To ignore such occurrences is to keep from providing Christian ministry to those in need. That is why Christians today need to know about deliverance. If a person is experiencing torments that do not seem to have an origin in the physical world, there may well be a demonic element at work.

EXTRAORDINARY POWER AND KNOWLEDGE

Extraordinary power and knowledge are commonly seen in those who are demonized. One Yoga guru could break strong chains through the power of the demonic. A slight teenaged girl could subdue several adults. A person levitating above a bed could not be restrained by four adults. It must be noted that unusual physical strength is often promised to those who will allow the demonic to enter them or who are unable to resist the demonic spirits indwelling them.

If a person has magical abilities, such as abilities to move objects through use of the mind alone or to cast spells on others for good or ill, such a person should be suspected of being empowered by demonic spirits. This sort of activity is common among those who practice Santería, Voodoo, Candomblé, Macumba, or Lukumi, all related.

On any number of occasions, I have been shocked, unnerved really, when a person undergoing deliverance suddenly begins to divulge things that happened in my life, things that I was embarrassed about and that this person could not have known. It was obvious that such things were intended to thwart the deliverance session, and I must report that the demonic strategy proved effective several times. Those who engage in deliverance work are sinners, of course, and there were times even after being born again when we experience failures.

It is sometimes quipped that the demonic kingdom has the second-best computer in the universe and has "files about us stored on hard drives," and the demons love to divulge these to prevent being cast out. It is an advantage to be aware of this ahead of time. Therefore, my counsel is to ignore the revelations coming from a demon and order it to "shut up."

Being attacked by a person when a demonic spirit was threatened with expulsion is common. Though I was never physically injured, still many battles took place, and this was almost always due to the person being ministered to not taking a stand against the indwelling demons. It is not uncommon for an evil spirit to recount to their host what goodies they would miss, if they, the demons, were cast out. It is imperative that the one with demonic spirits must want them out. We must keep in mind James 4:7: "Submit yourselves therefore to God. Resist the devil, and he will flee from you."

I cannot help the fact that some of the things I am saying here are rather hard to believe. Yet, it is crucial to describe some of the bizarre events that have taken place. It is essential to understand some of the crazy things that happen in deliverance work, lest beginners be frightened or confused.

Extreme Bondage to Sin

Uncontrolled addictions of any kind (from tobacco to heroin) and totally untamed lusts may indicate that one is demonized. Many of us have slight addictions (such as coffee), but when someone becomes totally and hopelessly addicted, dependent upon something or other, it could indicate the presence of the demonic.

This is true of lust. All of us have lustful thoughts from time to time, but when one finds that he or she is completely bound by lust, this could indicate the need for deliverance.

Demonization and Mental Illness

It is not always easy to tell the difference between mental illness and demonization, and they may be found together. One must therefore be very careful to distinguish between demonization and mental illness and not do anything that would further damage those with a mental illness.

It is not possible for most of us to drop everything and enroll in a university to study psychology. My goal had been to be a school psychologist, and I spent four years in such study between U.C. Davis and Sacramento State, yet now my knowledge from that era is mostly outdated, so I continue to study abnormal psychology. I urge all who would engage in deliverance ministry to learn as much as you can on the subject, reading at least a book or two.

I am not an expert on mental illness. Although my undergraduate degrees are in psychology, and for ten years I operated a counseling center, again I say I am no expert.

That said, here are a couple of clues for telling the difference between actual demonization and mental illness. It is much more common for the mentally ill to complain of being demonized than it is for the demonized to make such complaints. It seems that some mentally ill people may blame demonic forces for their troubled living. This is usually not true of those who are actually demonized. These genuinely demonized individuals may even be aware of the demons indwelling them. However, I have encountered scores of demonized people who didn't even believe in demons!

Those who are mentally ill will not generally react as violently to the Bible, the cross, prayers, or other religious objects as the demonized may.

With many forms of mental illness, people are divorced from reality. They may not know who they are or where they are. This is seldom true of the demonized. The mentally ill may be somewhat cut off from life and unable to care for themselves in many cases. The demonized most often can continue to operate in the physical world, but there is a change in the personality that cannot be explained. Here I am on touchy ground, because so very often some form of mental problem is combined with the demonic. One thing is clear: A mental illness cannot be cast out.

Engaging in deliverance ministry requires patience and loving care. It takes time and experience to become confident in this work. Not everyone is fit for this ministry; in fact, few will want to venture into this work.

I have found that the following questionnaire is helpful in discerning satanic influence. Here I suggest that the questionnaire be used in the early stages of working with a person who is seeking deliverance.

QUESTIONNAIRE FOR THOSE DESIRING DELIVERANCE

Have you ever...

Consulted (either in fun, out of curiosity, or in earnest):

Ouija board___ tea leaves___ crystal ball___ Tarot cards___ I Ching___ Mediums___ Psychics___

Played with games of an occult nature such as:

ESP___ Telepathy___ Mind Reading___

Sought, or been subjected to, as a child or adult, healing through magic conjuration and charming, such as:

A spiritualist___ Life Coach___ Christian Scientist___ shaman___ psychic healing___ hypnotherapy___ metaphysical healing___ use of the pendulum trance for diagnosis___ Reiki therapy___

Sought to locate missing persons or objects by consulting someone with psychic, clairvoyant, or psychometric powers?

Yes___ No___

Practiced table tipping (lifting)___ levitation___ or automatic (spirit) writing___?

Been given or worn an amulet, talisman or charm for luck or protection?

Yes___ No___

Practiced (or hired someone else to do) water witching (sometimes called dowsing or divining for water, etc.) using a twig or pendulum?

Yes___ No___

Visited an acupuncturist?

Yes___ No___

Read or possessed occult or spiritualist literature such as:

Books on astrology___ Interpretation of dreams___ Metaphysics___ Course in Miracles___ self-realization___ Fortune-telling___ magic___ ESP___ clairvoyance___ Psychic phenomena___ and especially occult magical books, such as "Secrets of the Psalms"___ or the so-called Sixth and Seventh Books of Moses___?

Experimented with or practiced ESP___ telepathy___ martial arts___?

Practiced any form of magic charming or ritual?

Yes___ No___

Do you possess any occult or pagan religious objects, relics or artifacts, which may have been used in pagan temples and religious rites, or in the practice of sorcery, magic, divination or spiritualism?

Yes___ No___

Have you had your handwriting analyzed___ practiced mental suggestion___ cast a magic spell___ or sought psychic experience___?

Have you practiced any form of Buddhist meditation?

Yes___ No___

Have you "awakened your kundalini" or received a guru's shaktipat?

Yes___ No___

Have you now or ever had a "spirit guide"?

Yes___ No___

Have you ever seen or been involved in Satan worship?

Yes___ No___

Are you now or have you ever been a practicing witch?

Yes___ No___

Have you had an imaginary playmate?

Yes___ No___

Have you used crystals for healing?

Yes___ No___

GROUPS

Circle any groups with which you have been connected (directly or indirectly):

Hare Krishna	Scientology
Zen Buddhism	Meher Baba
Rosicrucianism	Mormonism
Christian Science	Baha'i
The Third Way (Gurdjieff)	Unity
Unitarianism	Jehovah's Witnesses
TM	Unification church (Moon)
Children of God	Theosophy
Inner Peace Movement	Reiki
Spiritual Frontiers Fellowship	Religious Research of American
EST	The Way
Course in Miracles	Enneagram
Native American Church	Sufism
Kaballah	Santería

DRUGS

Are you, or have you been, a drug user or dealer of (Please circle for yes):

LSD	Psilocybin (Magic Mushrooms)
Peyote	Ayacucho
STP	Heroin
Morphine	Methedrine
Amphetamins (uppers)	Nembutal (downers)
Marijuana	Hashish
THC	Cocaine
Pain killers (addiction)	Glue sniffing
Opiods	Other _____

Have you ever experienced . . .

A strong sense of condemnation or debilitating guilt? Yes___ No___

Sexual abuse? Yes___ No___

Fear of committing the "unpardonable sin"? Yes___ No___

Pornography fascination? Yes___ No___

Describe other issues that come to mind in this regard:

SPIRITUALISM

Have you ever attended a "development circle?" Yes___ No___

Do you have a spirit guide? Yes___ No___

Do you have an animal spirit? Yes___ No___

Are you a practicing medium? Yes___ No___

Have you attended a séance? Yes___ No___

Have you visited a psychic, palm–reader, or crystal–ball gazer? Yes___ No___

Consulted with a "Life Coach" Yes___ No___

Other "Christian" variants:

Been "drunk" or "slain" in the Spirit? Yes___ No___

Received the "anointing"? Yes___ No___

Worshiped or communicated with Saints or Angels? Yes___ No___

Heard a "word from the Lord"? Yes___ No___

Practiced "contemplative prayer" or "soaking prayer"? Yes___ No___

**This questionnaire may be downloaded or printed by going to:
earthenvesselmedia.com/Deliverance**

Use the next page for Other Notes:

Other Notes:

CHAPTER EIGHT

HOW TO DO DELIVERANCE

JESUS IS THE DELIVERER

Deliverance is a ministry in which we engage, yet the resulting freedom from demonic oppression is accomplished by Jesus. Paul speaks of this human/ divine interaction in Colossians 1:29: "To this end I labor, struggling with all the energy he so powerfully works in me." We are pursuing the ministry, but Jesus is the true deliverer. Retaining this truth prevents anxiety and fear from hindering the deliverance ministers and gives the person being ministered to a sense of security and confidence.

Jesus cast demons out as a normal part of His overall ministry. He can be counted on to faithfully discharge this same ministry today, though not in person; thus, He has given us the authority to stand in His place and speak His name.

Our place of authority is in the victory of Christ. This is wonderfully stated in Colossians 1:15–20:

> [15] He is the image of the invisible God, the firstborn of all creation. [16] For by him all things were created, in heaven and on earth, visible and invisible, whether thrones or dominions or rulers or authorities— all things were created through him and for him. [17] And he is before all things, and in him all things hold together. [18] And he is the head of the body, the church. He is the beginning, the firstborn from the dead, that in everything he might be preeminent. [19] For in him all the fullness of God was pleased to dwell, [20] and through him to reconcile to himself all things, whether on earth or in heaven, making peace by the blood of his cross.

We enjoy the very same authority over evil spirits that the early disciples experienced. The Twelve (Luke 9:1, 2 and Matthew 10:1) and the seventy-two were given authority to cast out demons (Luke 10:17–19). Saints today have the same privilege. Our Lord says to us, "I have given you authority to trample on snakes

51

and scorpions, and to overcome all the power of the enemy; nothing will harm you" (Luke 10:19). But lest we become overly excited by this spiritual authority, Jesus gives this caution: "However, do not rejoice that the spirits submit to you, but rejoice that your names are recorded in heaven" (Luke 10:20).

Once, at the conclusion of a particularly successful deliverance, I was feeling quite exhilarated by the experience of seeing God's power in action. The very next deliverance (which followed within the same hour as the first) was a different story. It was like a car running out of gas. No power, no authority—just arguing, frustration, and a hoarse throat.

Humility is an essential quality for those doing deliverance. Without it, we are likely to be standing in our own power, which is insufficient against the hosts of darkness.

PREPARATION OF THE MINISTER

Of first consideration, we want to be **confident in our position in Christ**, as expressed in Ephesians 2:6: "And God raised us up with Christ and seated us with him in the heavenly realms in Christ Jesus."

Second, we hope to be **spiritually mature**. In a church I pastored in the 1970s, several young people were active in casting out demons. They had been trained and equipped to do it, they demonstrated consistent growth, and they were anxious to serve God. They hopefully grasped the great secret of resting in Christ according to Hebrews 4:1–11.

No one should do deliverance who is merely curious about it; it is not a spectator sport. Deliverance is serious business, and only those who are willing to pay the price should be allowed to minister in this area.

Demons are awful and easy to hate, but when their hideousness is manifest through a person, **care must be exercised not to be grieved at the person rather than the demon**. We want to keep in mind that we are wrestling against demonic principalities and powers and not against flesh and blood. We are to love the demonized and hate the evil one.

An important reminder here: **deliverance sessions can be extremely frustrating**, especially when they last for hours. Not all deliverances are the same. Some may be rapid and simple; others may be drawn out and taxing.

Fasting is optional, not a requirement—frankly, I rarely fasted. Some will refer to Mark 9:29 on this point. Here is the King James Version of this verse: "And he said unto them, this kind can come forth by nothing but by prayer and fasting."

Notice now the ESV of the same verse: "And he said to them, 'This kind cannot be driven out by anything but prayer.'" The reason for the absence of "and fasting" is because in the oldest and best manuscripts this phrase is missing. Imagine, being in a situation where deliverance was needed, and there was no time to fast.

Persons undergoing deliverance may be fearful and anxious. Anticipation of the unknown, particularly having to do with spiritual realms and the devil, can be extremely unnerving. One who casts out demons will hope to convey confidence, hope, and victory. I must state, that in most instances, those we worked with were so anxious to be freed from the demons that they were usually quite calm and relaxed. But not always so.

BUILD A TEAM—DELIVERANCE WORK CAN BE MESSY

Deliverance work should hopefully not be a solitary enterprise. While one person can do this, it is not safe or sane to do so on a regular basis.

As pastors, with numbers of others available for training to do this ministry, it can still be a daunting task. Make no mistake—it is tiring work, and those in need seem to sprout out of the woodwork. Any notoriety about someone so engaging in deliverance work could easily attract more desperate people than a single person, even a team, can deal with.

Notice the word "desperate" in the previous paragraph. People hoping to have demons cast out may have a deep sense of dread within them. Here they are with unclean, evil spirits inside their bodies and minds, and they may be experiencing all sorts of terrors, from which they have no escape. Those of us in this highly important service must recognize how crucial we become in these people's lives.

The team: at least two, better three, four, or more. As a long–time baseball coach I know the importance of the dynamics that go on in a team. The tighter the team, the better is the play. Perhaps one member is commanding demons to come out, maybe two, which is preferable. Then there are other team members present who are in prayer. In long drawn-out sessions, those commanding demons out will switch with the prayer warriors, and vice versa.

"Messy" is often a characteristic of deliverance work. Sometimes the unclean spirits come out fairly simply. Other times, with great difficulty. Much of this depends on a person's undergoing deliverance ability to submit to God and resist the demons before they flee. Real, wild, spiritual battles often go on inside a person indwelt with demons, which will do anything possible to avoid being evicted. Going on, and usually unknown to those commanding the evil spirits out, is a battle royal with lies and threats being streamed from the demons to their host.

I have found it **unwise to engage in physical struggles with a person undergoing deliverance**. Danger lurks here. I will state that I have never been injured in a spiritual/physical battle, but such could happen, and this is why a release/waiver form must be signed. Most serious is that a person being thrown about by a demon may be injured. On at least one occasion I was forced to suddenly stop a deliverance session for the above reasons. Such can take place when the person being ministered to needs to do more serious work like learning to submit to God and resist the devil. In such situations, it is necessary to postpone or reschedule a session during which pastoral care is administered.

Another aspect of "messy" has to do with failures to see through to victory. It is not clear what the percentage is of these, but it might be in the double digits. Here it is where those of us doing this crazy work are most vulnerable and can feel like failures. At times I have questioned whether or not I was spiritually strong enough, or not properly trained, and so on. **It can be physically wearing, often resulting in bad dreams, a sense of lethargy, and other symptoms** related to being worn out and tired all the time. Yes, there is a price to be paid for doing such "glorious" work.

One last point: **deliverance ministers need to be periodically relieved of their work**, and this may be the number one reason for the building of a team. It is not advised to advertise that you and team are engaged in this work of casting out demons, because you may become a target of both those wishing to rid themselves of demons and perhaps of the demons themselves.

ENGAGING IN A PHYSICAL BATTLE

One thing I am certain about is that **physical battles must be avoided.** There is danger here: ambulances, police cars, hospitals, jails, and court rooms—and that's not all. And in some of the books I have been consulting lately have been accounts where people must be restrained and subdued. Yes, I have seen a few of these myself, and the cause was that I had not properly prepared those needing deliverance.

Most of these situations can be avoided with pre-deliverance counseling sessions, forms filled out such as you find in this book, prayers for forgiveness of sin, forgiving others we have issues with, and more. **Proper deliverance must be deliberate and planned out.** At least as best as possible.

A number of times in my research I came across accounts where people doing deliverance had to have several large, strong men present to prevent someone from committing violent acts, levitating, or attacking the folks leading the deliverance session. Again, this demonstrates a lack of adequate counseling.

A major point here: **unless a person undergoing deliverance is submitting themselves to God, and are resisting the devil, indicating this is someone**

who is born again of the Holy Spirit, there will be usually be no deliverance. Merely appealing for help to be rid of tormenting spirits is not enough. Remember the account where a demon was cast out, but then returned, knowing that there was an empty place to inhabit, and brought along seven worse demons for company.

Am I saying that non-Christians cannot have unclean spirits cast out of them? No, but **I do think that unless the Holy Spirit is present, re-possession is likely.** I think that the passage below, Matthew 12 :43–45, tells the story:

MATTHEW 12:43–45   RETURN OF AN UNCLEAN SPIRIT

[43] "When the unclean spirit has gone out of a person, it passes through waterless places seeking rest, but finds none. [44] Then it says, 'I will return to my house from which I came.' And when it comes, it finds the house empty, swept, and put in order. [45] Then it goes and brings with it seven other spirits more evil than itself, and they enter and dwell there, and the last state of that person is worse than the first. So also will it be with this evil generation."

ONLINE DELIVERANCE

We live in a "Zoom" or "Skype" or "Slack" world (and other online communication formats) while being "shut down" in a pandemic. We have decided to take advantage of these and do deliverance online, and even after we return to some semblance of normal, those who live far away will still need someone to turn to. By remote we can be there and so can you. Here I have a word based upon my experience.

On three occasions my wife and I have engaged in deliverance work via Zoom, once to a woman in northern Europe, the other to a young man on the East Coast, and the third to a woman in Virginia. We could not tell if the first two attempts were successful. That said, **online may well be the only way to approach the situation.** The third session was successful, at least as much as first sessions in person tend to be. The difference between the first two and the last one was the commitment to Christ. The first two were mostly desperate but unable to submit to God and resist the devil, as far as we could see. The last one had no trouble in this regard.

At this point, the following is how I would approach a request to remotely do deliverance ministry:

First, after a discussion of the situation, **begin with a counseling/educational process, and this consisting mainly with the reading of several books.** Two of these would be this book you are reading now, and the other my book, *Deliver Us From Evil: How Jesus Casts Out Demons Today.*

No, I am not trying to sell books. Another book would be my Th.M. thesis, published by Zondervan in 1973 and now republished by Earthen Vessel, entitled, *A Manual of Demonology and the Occult*. Another valuable book is *Demonic Foes: My Twenty-Five years as a Psychiatrist Investigating Possessions, Diabolic Attacks*, and the Paranormal by Richard Gallagher, MD. He is a Roman Catholic who has worked for years with official Catholic exorcists. It is easily the best book I have ever read on deliverance ministry. Still another book is *Deliver Us From Evil: A Pastor's Reluctant Encounters with the Powers of Darkness* by Don Basham. I strongly suggest these books be 'devoured' by any who would engage in deliverance ministry.

Second, after proper preparation has been made by means of reading some of the books mentioned above, is **engaging in conversation with the person about to go through deliverance by going over the "questionnaire" and the "list of occult practices."** This sets up the first round of actual deliverance, casting out the demons. And this may take a number of online sessions. We continue until no demons make their presence known.

Third, **several regularly scheduled online meetings need be made**. Phone calling is okay, but it is better to see a person's face and body posture. It is best to **begin with listening to the story the person has to tell.** Have a notebook and take notes, asking few questions, and merely restating what you have been told. You may ask details about the family, schooling, and so on without teaching, preaching, directing. Listen carefully.

During these meetings, **make it known that you are not the one casting out demons; rather, it is Jesus who does this.** We are only standing in His place, since He gave us His power and authority to act on His behalf. Make sure the person is not still holding out some reserve of thought that a so-called secular or occult "life coach" could do the same.

A key need for these meetings online is to **describe what the deliverance session will look like**, which begins with prayer, mostly having to do with confession of those things whereby Satan can access a person's life. This is how it starts, then a description of what you will do, commanding demons to come out while he or she, in a prayerful attitude, submits to Jesus and resists the unclean spirits.

Fourth, **encourage this person to find a local church**. Once found, ask the person for contact information with the pastor or other member of the church. This last point is perhaps the most important, as direct engagement with members of the Body of Christ is extremely essential. (I have found this fourth point to be time consuming and often frustrating.)

Finally, make sure the person has your contact information, especially the phone number, since gaining visual access to you is more difficult.

GROUP DELIVERANCE

Both Don Basham and Derek Prince conducted group deliverance meetings. Some of these were planned, others simply erupted at a worship service. In general, it went like this: during rather expressive worship, a number of worshippers would fall to the floor and make strange noises with flailing of arms and legs. What to do?

These brothers did one of two things. One, the preacher would ask those not manifesting to back up and pray for the power of the Holy Spirit to set those undergoing torment to be delivered. Two, those struggling were gathered up and ushered to a separate room where more controlled deliverance could be undertaken.

As best as I could discern, some demons were cast out.

Do I recommend group deliverance? To be honest, I have not made up my mind. If such were to erupt, then the leader must make a decision. Either stop it, if that is even possible, or begin commanding demons to come out. Like noted above, this work can be messy.

I hope this never happens to me, and I think it possible to so conduct a service that there would not be such an outbreak.

Would I voluntarily attempt to conduct group deliverance? Not unless extreme circumstances demanded it. After all, what about aftercare and biblical counsel?

We are dealing with principalities and powers under the command of the god of this world. Anything can happen. We can at least be aware that things can happen and not be completely thrown off guard, if things turn ugly.

PREPARATION FOR PERSONS SEEKING DELIVERANCE

Once again, I suggest that **deliverance is best accompanied by counseling**. I recommend two counseling sessions (with more sometimes necessary). This is where the lists detailing occult involvement are filled out and discussed.

It takes time to build up a trust relationship between two people. Each possible avenue of invasion from the demons must be dealt with. Anyone who balks at counseling and wants immediate deliverance may be disappointed. Nevertheless, there have been numbers of occasions when it was apparent that immediate action had to be taken, thus no chance for a counseling session. Still there is a healthy flow to the ministry that helps to rightly prepare a person; short circuiting this should be avoided.

Thorough repentance is essential. Demons may cling to any hidden or unconfessed sin. Satan derives his authority in our lives from sin. When we walk in darkness, Satan and his hosts are there; as we walk in the light (free from sin), we have fellowship with Christ. The devil is stripped of any leverage he may have over us, as we claim the forgiveness the Father has given us in Christ.

In Acts 19:18–20, we find revival producing a rejection of the occult. Paul's work in Ephesus—the miracles, the preaching—yielded an abundant harvest. In that city were many who practiced witchcraft. Upon conversion, they rejected their past sins publicly.

> [18] Also many of those who were now believers came, confessing and divulging their practices. [19] And a number of those who had practiced magic arts brought their books together and burned them in the sight of all. And they counted the value of them and found it came to fifty thousand pieces of silver. [20] So the word of the Lord continued to increase and prevail mightily.

All association with the occult should be rejected. Books on the occult, ESP, fortune telling, meditation, magic, etc., should be discarded. Any trinkets or jewelry with magical significance should also be thrown away. It is better for this material, however valuable, to end up at the garbage dump than in a second-hand store or in the home of a friend or relative. Burn it if necessary.

Each area of occult involvement and excessive sin should be confessed and forgiveness asked for. It is best not to rush this part of the deliverance process.

If a person coming for ministry is not a Christian, this will be problematic at best. The vast majority of those desiring riddance of evil spirits are Christians. Several times when a non–Christian was so tormented that he or she sought help from Christian ministers, the results were not favorable. Yet, for a person who recognizes a demonic presence and is willing to submit himself or herself to Christ, deliverance is possible.

This is the natural order for freedom in Christ according to **James 4:7: "Submit yourselves, therefore, to God. Resist the devil, and he will flee from you."** Memorization of this verse is helpful. First comes submission to God. Only then can he or she resist and flee from the enemy.

It is important that anyone seeking deliverance be serious about following Jesus. Occasionally, people will request deliverance, because Satan is tormenting them, and ending this is the chief goal. This is an understandable reason, but it is not enough. If relief is all that is sought, the person will not be able to withstand subsequent attacks. Affirmation of a commitment to turn one's whole life over to Christ is critical.

Every violent deliverance I have experienced has been with a person who was either not fully committed to Christ or who was not resisting the devil. One young man became so enraged, I was forced to calm him down and end the ministering. On questioning him, he admitted that he had not thrown away his occult books and did not like coming to church because of the "hypocrites." Rebellion in that young man prevented him from becoming free. In the end, he walked away, keeping his demons and his stubborn attitude. As a rule of thumb, it is best to **do deliverance only with those who are dead earnest about living a Christ-centered life.** In any case, if we did deliverance on those who do not repent of their sin, the demonic spirits would very likely return. Here is how Jesus put it:

> [24] "When the unclean spirit has gone out of a person, it passes through waterless places seeking rest, and finding none it says, 'I will return to my house from which I came.' [25] And when it comes, it finds the house swept and put in order. [26] Then it goes and brings seven other spirits more evil than itself, and they enter and dwell there. And the last state of that person is worse than the first." Luke 11:24–26

THE PROCESS OF DELIVERANCE

It is preferable to do deliverance **in a quiet and private place.** A team of us were ministering one evening to a man, and the demons were coming out with screams. This went on for the space of an hour. We were startled by a light flashing through a window. It was a policeman. A nearby resident had heard the screaming and phoned the police. It was somewhat difficult explaining to the officer what we were doing!

It is recommended there be **two people minimum present** doing the ministry. If ministering to a woman, *always* have a woman present. This should be considered mandatory. On more than one occasion there was a partial disrobing and a little more; we must be prepared for such.

When those who attempt to do the work of deliverance are ill prepared for it, are excitable, immature in Christ, and fearful, difficulties can result. **Training to do deliverance work is necessary** and is essentially the "why" for this handbook.

It is good to **begin with prayer;** perhaps some **praise and singing, too.** The person being ministered to may then be **asked to renounce all occult practices and renounce Satan.** We ask God for victory and help in the work. This praying is out loud. During the counseling sessions that preceded the actual deliverance, the **entire procedure has already been explained,** so that nothing new is encountered. If there had been no time for counseling sessions, it would be good to carefully go over what will take place prior to the time of the deliverance.

**Here now is a story, one that involves speaking in tongues. In 1968, during my evangelism work in the Haight-Ashbury District of San Francisco, while I was camping at the Lincoln Park Baptist Church on Balboa Avenue between 41st and 42nd avenues, I woke up around 2 a.m. loudly speaking in tongues. And I was not a charismatic in the least; I was actually opposed to that. But there I was, and I didn't decide that it should happen; it just happened. I continued to speak in tongues until 1978, when it inexplicably ceased, and I have not done so since.

Anyway, at one deliverance experience, I was speaking in tongues when the person we were ministering to put his hands up to cover his ears and shouted out, "Stop that perfect prayer!" I was stunned, and I did not cease the tongue speaking. Then about one year later the exact same thing happened again.

Over the years, I rarely recounted these experiences. Then just a month ago, I read in Don Basham's *Deliver Us from Evil* his report of the same thing, and I mean the very same words by a person who shouted out while covering his ears, "Stop that perfect prayer!"

Needless to say, all three deliverance sessions went well.***

Back to working with a person just prior to a deliverance session: With good communication, the subject is then with you all the way. This is essential for a possible second step, commanding any demon to identify itself, when it would be typical to begin with, "Spirit, name yourself." Let me confess, that in going over this material for the re-publication of this book on deliverance, I realized we asked this question quite rarely. The reason was that I learned along the way that demons lie. Members of our deliverance team would often laugh and laugh thinking about the strange conversations we had with demons. I want to state right now that it is **unwise to engage in talking with demons beyond getting its identity or name**. It is best to command, "Be still." or, "Shut up."

A demon will fight fiercely; it does not want to be cast out. Jesus commanded a demon to name itself on one occasion. "Legion" was the name of that one. It appears that Jesus did not have to continually command demons out (they left with a word), but most often we need to repeat the command, sometimes over and over. Why Jesus was able to cast out all demons with one word and we are not, is not clear, except that we are not Jesus.

Again, it is not paramount to command a demon to name itself. Most of the time, I skip this point; however, on some occasions knowing the identifying name of a demon helped. Some of those who are experienced in deliverance work nearly always command a demon to name itself, which may help in having a better idea of how a demon may have affected a person's life. For instance, suppose a demon identifies itself as "hate." I need to be clear here: it is my opinion that demons do not actually have personal names. The name more likely describes how a spirit has worked or manifested itself. In the case of "hate," it may have been hate for parents, a wife or husband, a pastor, etc. This information may assist in bringing healing, forgiveness, and reconciliation.

Forgiveness is a key here. It is so very productive to help people identify those they have not forgiven, and once named, have prayer giving an opportunity to ask for forgiveness and extend forgiveness to others. Many who do deliverance work put a great deal of emphasis on this process.

A demon may name itself in one of two ways. It may be simply a name that seems to "run" through the mind of the person, or it may be more dramatic. Often, a demon will immediately manifest itself and scream its name at you. A third possibility is that the name will come to those ministering through either of the spiritual gifts, *knowledge* or *discernment.*

When a demon names itself, by whatever means, it is helpful to stop the deliverance and ask the person to reject the spirit and verbally order it to come out in the name of Jesus. At that point, the person needs to understand that a demon is a spirit and will come out as a "breath," through the mouth, usually in a scream, cough, sigh, or a simple exhaling.

Now the deliverance is beginning in earnest. **The ministers begin to command the spirit to come out.** Examples of this are: "We charge (command) you in the name of Jesus to come out "; "Spirit of _____, come out now in Christ's name": and "Demon, you are defeated, Jesus is Lord, and you must leave." "You demon are commanded to come out by Jesus Christ of Nazareth."

Such commanding may continue for some time. It may be asked, "Why more than one command?" The answer is simple – you discover that it is simply necessary. Deliverance ministry is imperfect as is every other kind of ministry. If each person were completely surrendered to God, fully resisting the devil, and if each minister were totally holy and filled with the Holy Spirit, deliverance would be incredibly simple.

A sense of relief may well follow a successful deliverance. As a demon leaves, perhaps in a scream as in Acts 8:7, a person will feel exhausted but peaceful. This is the chief way, other than discernment, that one has in knowing if actual deliverance has occurred. There is a release of tension and thankfulness to God for victory. **After one demon has gone, we continue until all are gone or exhaustion sets in.**

As a demon is being commanded to leave, strange occurrences may be seen. Once I, with several others, was ministering to a young woman who weighed about one hundred pounds. As the command to leave was spoken, the woman looked up with terrible rage on her face, sprang out of the chair, and pushed every one of us from our chairs. She grabbed a heavy table by one hand, lifted it, and threw it against the wall. At other times, demons have screamed (through the person's vocal cords), "I hate you," or "I will kill you." These tactics are used by demons to cause fear so that the deliverance will be halted. **All such outbursts are to be ignored.** As the deliverance proceeds, the extremes in behavior die down.

Those of us who do much deliverance work realize the **advantage of having others with us as we minister.** We will take turns and have rest periods when it drags on. It is usual for sessions to run for an hour or more. We do not expect to complete this ministry to a person the first time; **we suggest several one-hour sessions.** There are often two or three meetings, sometimes more, as we see the need. Hopefully, we quit only when no more demons are named or make their presence known. **But we will not go on day after day.**

Normally, deliverance sessions are carried out weekly. We do not rush through it and do not mind when weeks have gone by. Much healing can occur during these time intervals. We must not be compelled by a sense of urgency. In many years of such work, I have never lost even one person. There have not been any deaths, injuries, or insanities.

People often enjoy the attention they receive in deliverance. After three or four sessions, we may call a halt. If major spirits are cast out, other spirits will leave as a person seriously follows Christ. **It is not necessary to yield to every request for deliverance.**

SELF-DELIVERANCE

How about casting demons out of yourself? Is this even possible or recommended?

Don Basham, writing in the August 1972 edition of New Wine, states he cast demons out of himself. Here is what he wrote: "It was the realization that Christians, once they understand the principles involved, can call upon their Deliverer without the intervention of another human being at all. I had done this very thing when I was delivered first from the demon of Spiritualism, then from the spirit of fear: but somehow it had never occurred to me that this was a universal possibility."

Here is a prayer that he recommends:

Dear Lord Jesus Christ, I confess that I have sinned and as a sinner I deserve only Your judgment and not Your mercy. But I believe You died on the Cross for me and that You shed Your own blood for my sin. I hereby confess and repent of all my sins. (Be specific: name those sins known to you.) I ask You to forgive me. I accept Your sacrifice on the Cross for me. I accept You as my personal Lord and Savior and ask that You come into my heart and rule there. Thank You for forgiving me and saving me. I promise to live for You from now on. Thank You, Lord, Amen.

Following now are some other points from this article that may be of value regarding self-deliverance.

One, "I have found it essential to have every person seeking deliverance make a definite act of renunciation and dissociation from all forms of psychic and occult phenomena."

Two, "In most cases it seems that spirits must be dealt with one at a time. This means identifying the spirit, renouncing it, and commanding it to come out."

Three, "Physical symptoms which indicate the beginning of deliverance include shortness of breath, nausea, or a constricting of the throat, although deliverance may occur with none of these symptoms."

Four, "Then a few days later, additional symptoms may appear which indicate the presence of other spirits. This is a common occurrence, so there is no need for dismay or feeling that the spirits have returned."

There is no consensus on whether a person should attempt this while alone or not.

My evaluation of Basham's self-deliverance ideas is that it is legitimate. Sometimes there is no other alternative. However, it seems that a person would have to be a stable and a committed follower of Jesus to take this up.

SOME DON'TS

Do not argue or talk with demons. This is an error many of us made in the beginning. I have heard of people asking all kinds of questions of unclean spirits and believing them. Demons will sidetrack you if possible, to divert you from carrying out the work.

Do not believe demons. On one occasion a spirit said, "I'm out now." It was a lie, of course, and is quite characteristic of evil spirits. Many times, I have heard, "I am an angel," "I am Jesus," "Jesus is Lord," "I am the Holy Spirit," "I will not leave," "I am a good spirit," and many more. Never accept or deal with any comments. Rebuke and reject them all as if they had never been spoken and proceed with the ministry.

Demons may try to provoke you to anger. It is of no value to become angry at demons.

Lastly, do not give up easily. For reasons I cannot explain, deliverance may be a very slow process. Demons may even hide. The person undergoing deliverance may not know how things are progressing. He or she cannot be counted upon to give a reliable progress report. Persistence, patient endurance, and courage are excellent qualities for a deliverance minister to develop.

SPECIAL CIRCUMSTANCES

PEOPLE FROM OTHER CHURCHES

Normally I do not recommend doing deliverance with people from other churches. It is best if people seek ministry from their own pastor. However, if a person from another church comes for help, it is essential to secure permission from their pastor before proceeding. I have neglected this procedure to my regret.

CHILDREN

Deliverance for children is rare and not to be sought after, but if necessary, it should be conducted only with the parents' approval and in their presence. The same procedure is used with children as with adults, though care is taken not to frighten a child by loud voices.

A WIFE

Ideally the husband should know, lend his approval and permission, and be present if possible.

NEW BELIEVERS

It is best for a person to grow as a Christian before he or she receives deliverance. It will not hurt if it is delayed for some time. A new believer is not as able to submit to God and resist Satan as would a more mature Christian. Of course, this may not be possible for several reasons.

THE EMOTIONALLY DISTURBED

Usually deliverance, as far as I know, will not harm a person who is unstable emotionally when the work it is done with love and understanding. The name of Jesus has not been known to cause people harm. However, it is best to minister to those who are emotionally secure. If there is some doubt about the effects of the ministry, it is better not to do it.

THE OVERLY DEPENDENT

Due to the intensity of attention received in deliverance, dependent people often desire to continue going through deliverance long after it is warranted. A weaning process is necessary under such circumstances.

FINDING A CHURCH HOME

It is nearly impossible for anyone to find full deliverance without becoming part of a local church, Bible study, home group, or some other form of Christian fellowship. There is healing in the church, there is joy in knowing the brothers and sisters in the body, and one can learn to build confidence and faith by becoming a member of a local congregation.

PASSAGES FROM THE BIBLE TO BOTH KNOW AND HAVE MEMORIZED:

Isaiah 14:12-15

Matthew 12:45

Luke 4:5–6

John 10:10

John 14:30

2 Corinthians 4:4

Ephesians 1:20–21, 2:2, 3:10, 6:11–12

Colossians 1:13

James 4:7

1 John 3:8

Revelation 12:9, 12:12, 20:10

A CLOSING STORY

Somehow in the early 1970s, a brief mention of my involvement with casting out of demons came to the attention of someone at Time Magazine. This resulted in my receiving a phone call from a reporter with the magazine. I will call her Nancy, and she asked if she could attend a deliverance event. I said yes.

One dark and stormy November night I picked Nancy up at her apartment on Spyglass Hill in Greenbrae, Marin County, and we drove up to one of our Christian houses (communes) called Solid Rock on Wilson Avenue in Novato. Mark Buckley was the leader there, and we met for several years, usually on a Thursday, to do deliverance.

This was during the period when people were coming from near and far for this ministry, and appointments were set for this by workers at our Christian bookstores. It meant also that we did not know ahead of time whom we would be encountering.

Mark had created a space for our work in a large garage in the backyard of Solid Rock. Construction had not been completed, but Mark had fashioned a room in the upstairs with one single light bulb and a few chairs. There we were—Mark, Nancy, me, and the young man, whom I will call Jack, who was due for a deliverance session.

It was cold up there in the second story of an unfinished garage, and there the four of us sat. Mark and I faced each other, Nancy was on my right, and the young man on my left. He was about my age and build.

We went at the work as usual. We started with prayer, quoted a few Bible verses such as James 4:7, and began the commanding of demons to come out. Nancy sat there with a small notebook in her hands just watching and listening.

The subject sat in his chair silently, hands folded on his lap, head down, silent and calm. Mark and I went on with the work, commanding demons to come out, but there was nothing going on with Jack. We sang a song or two, spoke in tongues, and ordered demons out again, but nothing happened. We began to sweat despite the cold. (Later that evening, Mark and I talked together and felt for sure that Nancy considered us to be just religious idiots.)

But then, about an hour into it, things changed. Suddenly, Jack's chair crashed to the floor, he sailed straight up and back against the wall, which was about 10 to 12 feet behind him, and slid between the studs and hit the floor, hard. If the room had been finished with a ceiling, Jack would have collided with it.

Mark and I looked at each other with relieved looks on our faces. All right, the demons showed up! So we walked over, picked him up, and rearranged ourselves. I snuck a glance at Nancy who was now busy making notes. We simply continued, and in a short space of time, bam, chair down, Jack flying backward through the air, and bam on the floor again. This time Mark and I simply took our chairs over to the dazed Jack and cast out three or maybe more demons in short order.

Next up was a young woman, again about my age, and in less than a half hour several demons were cast out. No commotion, pure and simple.

When the Time Magazine issue came out, I anxiously read through Nancy's piece. Nothing, absolutely nothing of what happened that night at Deliverance Temple was there, the name we had given that garage. I called Nancy and asked what happened. She told me she submitted the story complete with what had happened, but an editor had said it was too fantastic and deleted the whole account. Oh well, but Mark and I realized later that this was perhaps the hand of God, for who knows what kind of chaos might have descended upon us if the account of the deliverance was broadcast all over America.

CHAPTER NINE

HINDRANCES TO DELIVERANCE

By hindrances I mean tactics that Satan employs to prevent or disrupt deliverance. The very instant demonization occurs, the invading spirits strive to remain in the person's body.

Hindrances may be simple (such as an uncontrollable temper) or complex (an extended intellectual debate). There will be hindrances in almost every deliverance session.

INTELLECTUAL HINDRANCE

DEMONS DO NOT EXIST

We know that Satan is a liar (John 8:44), and what better lie could he tell than that he and his unholy host are non-existent or fictional.

Demons will also hide, and this is very frustrating. There have been instances in which people have been terribly battered and abused, but with the beginning of deliverance all such demonic manifestations disappeared. "We are not here," is not a completely absurd statement for demons to make. Of course, if they are not there or are not real, they cannot possibly be cast out! It is not that the devil will attempt to deceive the deliverance ministers with such a foolish ploy, but rather, the target is the one needing Christ's power to be freed from the demons. Persons who should know of the reality of demons can at times deny their existence.

DEMONS ARE GOOD OR HARMLESS SPIRITS

Demons may claim to be angels or the spirits or souls of dead people. They also claim to be good not bad, whether angels or spirits.

White magicians, shamans, and witches will often speak of good spirits. They, of course, claim to traffic only with the good ones and avoid the evil ones. This is a deception, since there is only one good spirit, and that is the Holy Spirit; every other spirit is a demon. In a deliverance session I heard a demon make the plea, "Don't make me go; I'm a helping spirit." This is little more than an absurdity.

Very often, though, a person may believe a demon is necessary or good to have. One young man used demonic power to seduce women. He knew he was used by demons but wanted to keep them for what they could do for him. Other demons have so intertwined themselves into someone's personality that, due to insecurity, deliverance was resisted for fear of what life would be like without the demons. Shamanic practitioners may teach people to invite helpers into an imaginary dream house of the mind. These helpers are nothing more than demons. This has been demonstrated time after time in our ministry.

Demons are not good; they want to indwell and take "their" people's bodies right into hell so they can have them to live in forever. (Caution: please do not take the foregoing as necessarily biblically correct. Demons are liars, and anything one hears from one cannot be believed. But then again...)

GOD IS LOVE AND WOULD NEVER HURT EVEN A DEMON

This is a subtle hindrance, because it twists a spiritual truth — that God is love. The demons may put this thought into the mind of the one they indwell.

Now it is true that "God is love" (1 John 4:16), but it is also true that "the Lord your God is a consuming fire" (Deuteronomy 4:24; Hebrews 12:29). Since both Testaments teach that God is a God of fire as well as love, and that His judgment will fall on all who deliberately violate His Law. The Bible clearly teaches that God will judge the demonic. Jude 6 teaches this; 2 Peter 2:4 teaches this; and Jesus said, "Depart from me, ye cursed, into everlasting fire, prepared for the devil and his angels" (Matthew 25:41, KJV). Those angels that deliberately decided to rebel against God were cast out of heaven onto the earth and became what we know today as demons. They have been judged for their sin of rebellion. It is too late for them to repent. They chose to reject God's love, and now they await the eternal judgment (see Revelation 20:10–15).

As strange as it might seem, on several occasions I have heard demons say they have repented and turned from their evil ways. The implication, of course, is that they have earned the right to remain where they are.

Therefore, when a demon tells someone they indwell that "God is love, and would never hurt even a demon," we know that this is only a hindrance. It is a lie, because the Bible so clearly teaches the opposite.

DEMONS THAT ARE CAST OUT CAN REPOSSESS

It is true that demons can re-invade those from whom they have been cast out, but they can do this only under certain circumstances. Luke 11:24–26 explains this:

> [24] "When the unclean spirit has gone out of a person, it passes through waterless places seeking rest, and finding none it says, 'I will return to my house from which I came.' [25] And when it comes, it finds the house swept and put in order. [26] Then it goes and brings seven other spirits more evil than itself, and they enter and dwell there. And the last state of that person is worse than the first."

This is a *very* important passage of Scripture, for in it our Lord not only tells us that a person can be re-indwelt, He also tells us under what conditions this can occur. The described event is when, after demons are cast out, there is a spiritual vacuum. Then the spirit finds the body (house) "unoccupied" or "empty" (KJV). The Bible commentator R.C.H. Lenski says of this word in the original Greek:

> It is literally "at leisure" (or "standing empty"), nobody is occupying it. This is most significant. The Holy Spirit is not occupying the man and his heart. Why he (the Holy Spirit) is not is easily guessed. No true change has been wrought in him.

The passage teaches, then, that persons who have demons cast out of them become repossessed when the empty place in their being is not filled with the Holy Spirit. Demons can reenter only when people are not born-again followers of Jesus.

When demons put the idea in the person's mind who is about to be delivered that, "We will come back," it is partly true. They will come back if the delivered person is not converted.

But there is a warning in what Jesus taught in our passage. If a person fails to follow Christ, if he or she fails to turn from their sins that allowed the demons to enter in the first place, then he or she has deliberately re–opened his or her life to the demonic and may become even more demonized than before.

DEMONS CAST OUT WILL ENTER A LOVED ONE

Sometimes the demons will instill within the mind of those they indwell that if they are cast out, they will enter a member of the person's family, a spouse, a child, or someone else who is near and dear to them. Oddly enough, a demon may even threaten to enter a pet.

Demons are powerless when they are cast into hell. I say this based on several instances when I would say, "Jesus Christ of Nazareth casts you into hell." This almost always caused a ruckus. Demons would be instantly fearful and begin pleading not to be sent into hell. Strange as it may seem, early on I felt a certain sadness when a demon started begging. These evil spirits sometimes appeared to have graduated from theatrical school, they put on such a persuasive performance! What became clear because of this kind of hindrance is that hell is a real place into which even demons fear to be cast.

DEMONS THAT ARE CAST OUT WILL KILL OR HARM THE PERSON, THE MINISTER, OR A LOVED ONE

A bit more on this theme, since it pops up so regularly. This is nothing more than a hindrance, an attempt to put a thought into the person's mind that will make him or her stop going through deliverance. When the demons are bound in the name of Jesus, they can harm no one.

The motion picture, The Exorcist, did harm by seeming to show that the exorcist, the elderly priest, died as a result (direct or indirect) of his work against the demonic. During my years of doing deliverance, with literally scores upon scores of people, I have never had one incident in which the demons were able to touch us, the person undergoing deliverance, or anyone else. We bind them in Jesus' name, and they are powerless.

THERE ARE NO DEMONS PRESENT – IT IS ONLY PSYCHOLOGICAL

This issue is addressed several times in this handbook already, and I must confess it is a thorny issue, one which I do not fully understand. Even though my college degrees are in psychology and I operated a counseling ministry for ten years, I still cannot put all the pieces together. And yes, there were several instances when there was nothing demonic at all, at least as far as I could determine.

Merely mental issues? Could very easily be, but it would take a higher level of diagnosis skills than I possess to ascertain this. It could also have been that I became exhausted, frustrated, and simply ceased the work too early. Delivery ministry is not clean and simple.

Those of us doing this work have to go slow and be cautious. No one will become an expert in casting demons out of people just because or even when the need is desperate. Let me strongly suggest going slowly through the book, *Demonic Foes*. It is written by Richard Gallagher, an MD, who became a psychiatrist and published this book in October 2020. The subtitle of his book is, *My twenty-five years as a psychiatrist investigating possessions, diabolic attacks, and the paranormal.* Dr. Gallagher is a Roman Catholic and has been called in by official exorcists many times. My wife Katie and I devoured the book; it is the best book on the subject, in our opinion.

THE DEMONS ARE GONE

Once when casting out demons in the earlier days, when several demons had already come out, I asked a person if there were any more demons left. The response was, "We're gone." I came close to ending the session. Then I thought, "Wait a minute, if they're gone, how can they still be speaking through the person's mouth?" Of course, they were not gone; they were only pretending they were gone.

Most often, at the beginning of a deliverance session, all is calm, and no demons manifest themselves. Despite praying, quoting Scripture, and commanding demons to come out, nothing happens at all. The subject sits quietly and patiently, with head bowed and arms folded. I must admit I have been fooled into thinking that the demons were gone then, or that there were never any in the first place. What to do then?

If the subject is willing, we recommend that another appointment be made and that deliverance should continue, even if there are no demonic manifestations for the first time or two.

This is a good place for another story. It begins when our band Joyful Noise were asked to come to a large church in the East Bay. We met the pastor, who had heard of us and then invited us, and we quickly established a friendship. Some weeks later this pastor called and asked if he could bring his daughter over, since he thought she was having trouble with demonic spirits. I will call this fifteen-year-old Jane.

Jane's parents brought her to Deliverance Temple in Novato where Mark and company lived. Once per week for six weeks Jane's parents brought her over, and for six weeks Mark and I did our work, but no demonic spirit was encountered. Mark and I felt very badly about this and thought we had better let Jane's parents know that the sessions ought to end. Jane's father, the pastor, pleaded for one more time. We agreed.

Again, up in the loft of Deliverance Temple, Mark and I did our thing, and again, nothing at all. With heavy hearts we came back into the house, and our dear pastor friend prepared to have us share communion. First the bread, and the loaf went around the circle of us, about ten all together taking off pieces. Then the cup began making its way around. When it got to Jane, and as she was bringing it to her lips, she fell to the floor as in a swoon, with grape juice splashing about. Mark and I looked at each other, grinning now, came over to Jane lying on the floor, and in a few minutes, we cast about a half a dozen demons out of her.

A week later I got another call from our pastor friend who told us an interesting story. During the recent summer a couple dozen young people from his church traveled to Haiti to do mission type work. They returned with a young Haitian girl the same age as Jane. Little did the pastor or his wife know that after everyone had gone to bed, Jane and the guest would conduct Voodoo rites and rituals, giving a path of permission for the demons to enter Jane.

The pastor and his wife brought the Haitian girl over to Deliverance Temple a week or so later, and in rather short order, several demons were cast out of her.

Jane has bright red hair. Jumping ahead perhaps twenty years, I was sitting on one of the benches on the porch of our Miller Avenue Baptist Church in Mill Valley, just before the morning service, when a car drove up and stopped in front. I caught a glimpse of young read-haired kids sitting in the back seat. The driver's side door opened, and here came Jane. She rushed up to me, gave me a big hug and dashed back to her car.

GOD WILL NOT HELP BECAUSE YOU ARE TOO SINFUL

Another hindrance that demons often put into the mind of the one they indwell is, "You are too sinful; God has rejected you; He will not help you."

In these cases, John 3:16 and 1 John 4:9–10 may prove helpful in showing a person that God loves him or her, even though he or she is a sinner. John 3:18, "Whoever believes in him (Jesus) is not condemned," Is particularly helpful. "Christ Jesus came into the world to save sinners," (1 Timothy 1:15) is also helpful.

FEAR OF EMBARRASSMENT

Perhaps one of the primary reasons deliverance from evil spirits is difficult is due to the fear of being embarrassed by exposure of one's sinful ways. Who is not vulnerable to this fear?

On several occasions I was asked to do deliverance with pastors of churches. These wonderful pastors were scared to death of others finding out about their involvements, and especially of coming to me for help. Here I was, a very young man back in the 1970s, not a celebrity of any kind, but few were doing this work. I would commit to keeping everything a secret, and I have done so to this day.

A time or two, I made appointments with men, not knowing they were pastors who were using false names. This was doubly embarrassing, since I would eventually become aware of their real identities.

That is one side of it. The other is embarrassment just to confess actual, personal sin in front of others, and not only for pastors, but for all of us. How many wasted hours I spent attempting to cast out demons, when the work could have been radically shortened by openly admitting to involvement with sin, some deep and dark.

Who wants to admit especially to sexual sins, sometimes sin that, if known, may well have meant a jail sentence and professional ruin? We human beings can sink to low places. One might state, "Well, that was before I was born again." Still, it must be covered up, since the Christian community, or segments of it, can be very critical and harsh. Or it could be a lie to save face, and the sin might be current and under way at present. This fear of being exposed is extraordinarily powerful.

A deliverance team, for the reasons presented above, must be of high caliber and noted for their trustworthiness. I cannot state this more strongly: many people will never come to have tormenting demons cast out, because they know it would mean exposure of their sinful ways.

This very issue came up for me yesterday. A person was so very shy, he could not say what terrible sin he was involved in. When I started talking about the fear of embarrassment, especially when it came to sexual stuff, this man relaxed and confessed to a wide variety of depravity. Though at the very threshold of the deliverance, it seems highly likely to me right now that ministry to him will be successful.

HAVING A DEMON IS THE UNPARDONABLE SIN

Demons will sometimes tell the one they indwell that he or she has committed the "unpardonable sin," thus there is no use in seeking deliverance, since the sin of being demonized is that "unpardonable sin."

To counter this lie, we can explain just what the unpardonable sin is. Jesus said,

> I tell you the truth; all the sins and blasphemies of men will be forgiven them. But whoever blasphemes against the Holy Spirit will never be forgiven; he is guilty of an eternal sin. (Mark 3:28, 29)

This sin of blaspheming the Holy Spirit consists of continually rejecting His work. John 16:7–11 is clear on this point. When a person becomes completely hardened and unreceptive to the Holy Spirit, the person stops being at all interested in the Gospel. This person is then dead in sin. Anyone who is at all interested in being helped by Jesus *cannot* have committed this sin of rejecting the Holy Spirit. The very fact that someone has come for counseling and deliverance *proves* that he or she is still interested in becoming a good Christian. Thus, they could not possibly have committed the unpardonable sin.

Jesus said clearly in Mark 3:28, "all the sins and blasphemies of men will be forgiven them." This applies to all sins that bring about demonization as well. The "unpardonable sin" is rejecting Jesus all your life until you are dead. As long as men are still alive and have any interest in Jesus, they have not committed it.

DELIVERANCE WILL NO DOUBT FAIL, SO WHY TRY?

This hindrance from the demonic may come before any of attempts at deliverance or, more probably, after an unsuccessful deliverance session. The demons will tell the person there is no use in trying, since any deliverance attempts will fail. It is as if a demon whispered in this person's ear, "You are no good, you are hopeless."

I have seen this tactic used a moment or two before a dramatic deliverance took place. It is often a "last ditch" effort on the part of demons. The person needs to be made aware that this is often the case. It is also helpful to read a biblical case or two of the power Jesus has over the demonic, such as Mark 5:1–15 or Acts 16:16–18.

DELIVERANCE WILL CAUSE INSANITY

Persons who are highly emotional and insecure may be told by the demons that they will go insane if they experience deliverance. The person needs to be made aware that this is a rather stupid hindrance. Read to him or her the case in Mark 5:1–15 again. Stress the words in verse 15, "in his right mind." Contrast this with "night and day among the tombs and in the hills, he would cry out," in verse 5.

Jesus *delivers*. That is the *whole* point of it. Then, have him or her read 2 Timothy 1:7 for assurance.

JESUS CANNOT CAST DEMONS OUT

Sometimes demons will put this hindrance in a person's mind. The person will feel that Jesus is unable to accomplish this work. Again, explain that this is simply a lie. Speak of a case or two you know of in which demons were cast out (Perhaps one of the cases in the Bible or in this book). Then read Ephesians 1:10–22. Stress verses 20 and 21 over and over until the hindrance is seen for what it is — a lie! Jesus is above all powers, all demons, and Satan himself!

PHYSICAL AND EMOTIONAL HINDRANCES

There may be emotional or physical hindrances that accompany deliverance sessions. These are also meant to short circuit the process. The most common types include the following:

PHYSICAL UPSETS

The demons indwelling the person may try to stop the deliverance by bringing about physical distress. Included may be,

1.   Stomach pains
2.   Shortness of breath

3. Voices in the head (mind)
4. Pain in the chest
5. Pain in the throat
6. Pain in the back

One verse (James 4:7) may be used to help the person get through any or all of these physical upsets: "Submit yourselves therefore to God. Resist the devil, and he will flee from you."

Ask the person to repeat the verse. Ask him or her to resist giving into the pain or discomfort.

Explain carefully, that the demons can only cause discomfort, they cannot inflict lasting illness. Explain that these symptoms are merely used to divert the mind and produce fear.

Physical contortions

The demons will sometimes try to induce people to make ugly faces, or to contort their arms, legs, and body. The demons can also cause these phenomena to happen. "Resist" is what we find in James 4:7, but a person may not be able to do it. (This is a bit of a murky area, and we must remain flexible here.) At times I have commanded demons to leave the person alone or have stopped the session for a time and then speak to the person about the contortions to determine if they can resist them.

I admit this is another area where I wish I had it all figured out. It is easy to be confused about what to do. Probably, the physical contortions are caused by the demonic spirits, thus the necessity of continued commands for the demons to come out.

Violent actions

If violence does occur, and the person refuses to resist such impulses, the deliverance session is stopped. There may be exceptions to this on rare occasions, as when the person is too demonized to resist. These are very rare cases and should be dealt with differently. At this point, there is little counsel I feel confident to relate. Sometimes we simply must not proceed, in order to protect everyone involved.

To repeat—cases where violence erupts are rare. Chances are you will never encounter one. At the conclusion of this chapter is a "waiver" or "release" form that may be important to have the person being ministered to sign. During the 1970s the legal environment was quite lenient, but times have changed. We must be careful and prudent when it comes to the casting out of demons.

FEAR OF WASTING THE MINISTER'S TIME

This is a common emotional hindrance. Routinely it is good to inform the person undergoing deliverance that God has called *you* to the work of this ministry. It may be appropriate to state that you, not he or she, should decide if time is being wasted.

FEAR OF THE REACTION OF FRIENDS OR RELATIVES IF WORD GETS OUT

This is another common emotional hindrance that can easily be cleared up. Simply state that the deliverance sessions are *strictly* confidential. Then make sure they are! Make it a rule, and don't use deliverance sessions for illustrations in sermons.

SPIRITUAL HINDRANCES

All spiritual hindrances are removed when both the minister(s) and the person being ministered to are observing James 4:7: "Submit yourselves, therefore to God. Resist the devil and he will flee from you." This is probably the most important single verse in the New Testament on deliverance.

The great Reformer, Martin Luther, wrote:

And though this world, with devils filled,

Should threaten to undo us,

We will not fear, for God hath willed

His truth to triumph through us.

The prince of darkness grim –

We tremble not for him;

His rage we can endure,

For lo! His doom is sure

One little word shall fell him.

Did we in our own strength confide,

Our striving would be losing,

Were not the right man on our side

The man of God's own choosing.

Dost ask who that may be?

Christ Jesus it is He;

Lord Sabbath is His name,

From age to age the same,

And He must win the battle.

The form on the following page may be downloaded from earthenvesselmedia. com/Deliverance. Please be advised that this form is merely a suggestion and is not intended as legal advice or as a guarantee of no legal repercussions for anyone attempting to perform the ministry of deliverance.

DELIVERANCE MINISTRY RELEASE FORM

Due to the sensitive nature of what is commonly known as "deliverance minis-try," it is essential that anyone desiring this ministry sign a release.

There is no monetary cost for this ministry. It is offered as a pro–bono service of those ministering.

The ministry team will not publish, audio record, or video record the events of the deliverance session(s).

Our approach is very simple. We (at least two) will gather, and if the subject of the ministry is a woman, another woman will be present. We will begin with prayer, followed by confrontation of any demonic spirits present. They will be commanded to leave by means of the person and work of Jesus Christ.

This ministry is often unpredictable regarding how long it may take. It may be completed quickly or require a long course of time, with a series of ministry sessions necessary.

[]

I, the undersigned, have read the above and understand the process of the min-istry. I agree to release the ministry team from any liability, including, but not limited to, lack of success, mental or emotional distress, or physical distress.

Printed Name: _____

Signed: _____

Date: _____ At: _____

Witnesses:

_____

_____

CHAPTER TEN

THE GREAT RESISTANCE: THE TEMPTATION OF JESUS

LUKE 4:1–13 THE TEMPTATION OF JESUS[1]

[1] And Jesus, full of the Holy Spirit, returned from the Jordan and was led by the Spirit in the wilderness [2] for forty days, being tempted by the devil. And he ate nothing during those days. And when they were ended, he was hungry. [3] The devil said to him, "If you are the Son of God, command this stone to become bread." [4] And Jesus answered him,

"It is written, 'Man shall not live by bread alone.'"

[5] And the devil took him up and showed him all the kingdoms of the world in a moment of time, [6] and said to him, "To you I will give all this authority and their glory, for it has been delivered to me, and I give it to whom I will. [7] If you, then, will worship me, it will all be yours." [8] And Jesus answered him, "It is written,

"'You shall worship the Lord your God, and him only shall you serve.'"

[9] And he took him to Jerusalem and set him on the pinnacle of the temple and said to him, "If you are the Son of God, throw yourself down from here, [10] for it is written,

"'He will command his angels concerning you, to guard you,' [11] and "'On their hands they will bear you up, lest you strike your foot against a stone.'" [12] And Jesus answered him,

"It is said, 'You shall not put the Lord your God to the test.'"

[13] And when the devil had ended every temptation, he departed from him until an opportune time.

---

1   Matthew 4:1–11 also describes the Temptation of Jesus

The first temptation is "If you are the Son of God, command this stone to become bread."

The "if" here is a first-class conditional clause and would best be translated "since." This shows that the devil admitted Jesus is the Son of God. Jesus quotes from Deuteronomy 8:3, which says "Man shall not live by bread alone," thus refusing the devil's temptation. It is plain that the devil knows what is written in the Hebrew Bible, the Old Testament.

The second temptation is that the devil would give Jesus all the kingdoms of the world if He would "worship" him. Jesus then quotes Deuteronomy 6:13, which counters the offer and denies the devil's dare. If Jesus would have given in to the devil's temptation, His death on the cross would not have been sufficient to atone for sin.

The third temptation begins with "If you are the Son of God, throw yourself down from her." As in the first temptation, the "if" is a first-class conditional clause and again could or should be translated "since." The devil, of course, knows who Jesus is and hopes that, were Jesus to throw Himself down, it would result in serious injury or death, would be a direct violation of the Holy word of God, and would thus make Jesus a sinner and preclude His dying on the cross as the *sin-less* Lamb of God. Jesus resists again and quotes Deuteronomy 6:16 which reads, "You shall not put the LORD your God to the test."

Did the devil actually think Jesus would break the Word of God and commit sin? The answer must be "yes!" And how could this be? The clear biblical truth is that Jesus "emptied Himself and took on flesh." John 1:1 has, "In the beginning was the Word, and the Word was with God, and the Word was God. (The word "was" is a conjunction that does not connote time thus it could be translated, "was and is.")

And then in Philippians 2:5–8 we find Paul's way of stating the humanness of Jesus:

> [5] Have this mind among yourselves, which is yours in Christ Jesus,
> [6] who, though he was in the form of God, did not count equality with
> God a thing to be grasped, [7] but emptied himself, by taking the form
> of a servant, being born in the likeness of men. [8] And being found in
> human form, he humbled himself by becoming obedient to the point of
> death, even death on a cross.

Though Christians have struggled to understand the God/Man over the centuries and find a neat and tidy way to express it, we simply come to the place where we see the Scripture is clear as to who Jesus is—He is both God and man at once. The devil certainly knew it, that there was the potentiality for Jesus to yield to temptation. If such were not possible, if there were no humanness in Jesus, He would simply be God is disguise.

A couple of other points here before moving on: One, in verse 5 we find something rather incredible: the devil "took him up and showed him all the kingdoms of the world in a moment of time." The word time here is *chronos*, meaning ordinary time, like clock time. Right there and then, the devil was able to show Jesus all the kingdoms of the world. Think then of the powers of Satan to dazzle potential devotees. We cannot underplay or understate the dramatic and miraculous powers of Satan. And it is Satan's other-worldly power and knowledge that attract so many.

Satan promised that if Jesus would worship him he would give all these kingdoms to Jesus. Now what does the Scripture say of Satan? In John's Gospel, chapter 8, we find Jesus locked into an argument with Pharisees, a leading sect in Judaism. At one point, Jesus said to them:

> You are of your father the devil, and your will is to do your father's desires. He was a murderer from the beginning, and has nothing to do with the truth, because there is no truth in him. When he lies, he speaks out of his own character, for he is a liar and the father of lies. (John 8:44)

The devil is a liar, and he does not give what he promises those who submit to him; indeed, he cannot. But the lure is too much for too many. Wealth, power, knowledge, sex to the excess, and the ability to amaze and deceive—too strong for many of us.

We are to resist the temptations offered to us by Satan and his minions, the demons. One of the most important verses in the Bible is James 4:7: "Submit yourselves therefore to God. Resist the devil, and he will flee from you." Whenever we have struggled and failed in assisting someone to be free from demonic control, the root cause has been an unwillingness to take a firm stand against Satan and his demons. Without resisting Satan there will be no deliverance. Often it has been that a person comes seeking to have demons cast out due to the horrors they are experiencing, only to be told by these demons what they will lose if they are cast out. We have seen this countless times.

One story comes to mind. About seventeen years ago, I received a call from a young man who lived across the street from a supermarket. For years, spirits abiding in him would instruct him to cross the street, enter the market, go to a certain aisle, and there would be a young woman whom he could take to his apartment for the night. And so it went, but the price this fellow was paying was driving him mad.

He called for an appointment, came to my office, and the man who will be called

Bill told his story. Now Bill was not a Christian. I began to command any unclean spirits to come out, and nothing seemed to be working, despite the prayers and bits of counsel over the course of about one-half hour. Finally, Bill stopped, looked up, and simply said that if the spirit were cast out, he would get no more women at the market. With that, he stood up and walked out the door.

The lure of sexual excitement was too much for Bill to give up. The demons lied to him and dangled sex before him. The typical result would be chaos in his life and finally being trapped in hell for eternity. Not a good bargain.

We are each called to commit ourselves to God and resist the devil.

CHAPTER TEN

HOW TO MAINTAIN DELIVERANCE

T hose engaged in ministering deliverance need to help those who have been delivered to maintain their freedom from Satan.

Here are three key elements in maintaining our freedom in Christ: (1) abide in repentance; (2) abide in Christ's victory (3) and abide in Christ's church.

ABIDE IN REPENTANCE

It is part of the normal Christian life that we repent, that is, in prayer confess our sin and ask for forgiveness. This important principle is found in 1 John, as well as other places in the Scripture. We are to repent of our sin, which we need to do daily.

We need to be clear here: If someone has had demons cast out of them, they are not going to be re-demonized when a sin is committed. It would take direct and willful engagement with demonic practices for this to occur and is questionable even then.

Hebrews 12:1 gives us the pattern for Christians to follow: "Therefore, since we are surrounded by such a great cloud of witnesses, let us throw off everything that hinders and the sin that so easily entangles, and let us run with perseverance the race marked out for us."

Abiding in repentance is perhaps most clearly taught in 1 John 1:5-2:6. The main points of the passage are these:

1. How to walk in the light, 1 John 1:5-7

2. What to do if you sin, 1 John 2:3-6

3. Obey to avoid sinning, 1 John 2:3-6

The following verses are particularly important, and each one who has had deliverance should be made aware of them:

83

The blood of Jesus, his Son, purifies us from every sin (1 John 1:7).

This verse will help people to see Christ's blood as the only remedy for every sin. This points out that when Jesus died on the cross for us, He shed His blood, and it is this cleansing, this washing away of all sin, past, present, and future, that brings us forgiveness.

The next verse, 1 John 1:9, gives us great promise:

> If we confess our sins, he is faithful and just and will forgive us our sins and purify us from all unrighteousness.

1 John 2:4–6 shows us how to avoid such sins, by obeying the commandments of Christ:

> [4] Whoever says, "I know him," but does not keep his commandments is a liar, and the truth is not in him, [5] but whoever keeps his word, in him truly the love of god is perfected. By this we may be sure that we are in him: [6] whoever says he abides in him ought to walk in the same way in which he walked.

ABIDE IN CHRIST'S VICTORY

To be able to avoid the devil, the delivered person will learn to remain in the victory of Christ: Here is John 15:4–5:

> [4] Abide in me, and I in you. As the branch cannot bear fruit by itself, unless it abides in the vine, neither can you, unless you abide in me. [5] I am the vine; you are the branches. Whoever abides in me and I in him, he it is that bears much fruit, for apart from me you can do nothing.

Another verse that is particularly helpful is 1 John 4:4:

> You, dear children, are from God and have overcome them, because the one who is in you is greater than the one who is in the world.

These are dear and precious passages, and it is best to memorize them so that they will come up for us in times of need.

Christ is Lord. We have the greatest power in the universe, the power of Christ, within us. As we grasp hold of this reality, we learn we can never be defeated by the enemy! This is plain in the following verses from Paul:

> If God is for us, who can be against us? . . . Who shall separate us from the love of Christ? Shall trouble or hardship or persecution or famine or nakedness or danger or sword? . . . No, in all these things, we are more

than conquerors through him who loved us. For I am convinced that neither death nor life, neither angels nor demons neither the present nor the future, nor any powers, neither height nor depth, nor anything else in all creation, will be able to separate us from the love of God that is in Christ Jesus our Lord. (Romans 8:31,35,37,39)

There are other helpful verses that reference our abiding in Christ:

2 Timothy 1:7; Proverbs 3:5,6; Psalm 108:13; Psalm 27:1; Psalm 27:14; Psalm 46:1,2; and Isaiah 26:3,4. I consider Philippians 4:13 to be among the very best: "I can to all things through him who strengthens me."

The Scripture declares, "Thy word have I hid in my heart, that I might not sin against thee" (Psalm 119:11, KJV). There is nothing like memorizing the promises in God's Word and repeating them daily to develop one's ability to abide in Christ's victory.

ABIDE IN CHRIST'S CHURCH

To maintain deliverance, it is essential that we become a committed member of a local church.

The Bible tells us of those who were converted on the Day of Pentecost:

So those who received his word were baptized, and about three thousand were added to their number that day. And they devoted themselves to the apostles' teaching and to the fellowship, to the breaking of bread and the prayers. (Acts 2:41–42)

The word "church," based on the Greek meaning of the word, refers to those who have been called out from the world and who now belong to Christ, who gather together in community to worship, have fellowship, and live a life of being a follower of Jesus. Everyone born again of the Holy Spirit has meaning, purpose, community (fellowship), and a pattern of worship and observance. Below is what that first grouping of believers in Jesus actually did:

1.   Attended Bible studies, Acts 2:42 (the apostles' doctrine)

2.   Were together, had fellowship, Acts 2:42

3.   Attended communion, the breaking of bread, Acts 2:42

4.   Attended prayer meetings, Acts 2:42

5.   Regularly attended gatherings of the Church, Acts 2:46

6.   Had fellowship in their homes, Acts 2:46

Scripture says, "Let us consider how we may spur one another on toward love and good deeds. Let us not give up meeting together, as some are in the habit of doing, but let us encourage one another – and all the more as you see the Day approaching" (Hebrews 10:24,25).

As the "Day" of Christ's Second Coming approaches, there is an increasing need to remind followers of Jesus to "spur one another on" and encourage them not to "give up meeting together." Christian TV and radio are wonderful in their place, but they can never build the strong personal bonds of fellowship necessary for victory over Satan. The local church — this is a major key to successful Christian living!

In Romans 1:6, we find Paul speaking of local churches in his own day:

> I commend to you our sister Phoebe, a servant of the church in Cenchreae (Romans 16:1). Greet Priscilla and Aquila. Not only I but all the churches of the Gentiles are grateful to them (Romans 16:3,4). Greet also the church that meets at their house (Romans 16:5). All the churches of Christ send greetings (Romans 16:16). The God of peace will soon crush Satan under your feet (Romans 16:20).

SUMMING UP

To keep deliverance, to maintain victory over Satan, it is important to alert everyone to these important areas:

1. Speak to everyone on how to repent and come back to Christ when they sin, 1 John 1:9,7

2. Speak of how to remain in Christ's victory, Philippians 4:13; 1 John 4:4

3. Speak of the importance of being filled with the Spirit, Ephesians 5:18; Psalm 51:1–13.

4. Speak of the importance of becoming and remaining a functioning member of a local church, Hebrews 10:24,25; Acts 2:42.

Timothy Dwight, Jonathan Edwards' grandson, and president of Yale University, wrote:

> I love Thy kingdom, Lord,
> The house of Thine abode,
> The church our blest Redeemer saved
> With his own precious blood.
> For her my tears shall fall;
> For her my prayers ascend;
> To her my cares and toils be given,
> Till toils and cares shall end.
> Beyond my highest joy
> I prize her heavenly ways,
> Her sweet Communion, solemn vows
> Her hymns of love and praise.

It is my fondest hope that this handbook on deliverance will be used by God to help the churches of Christ.

DELIVERANCE AND THE OCCULT

BY ROBERT STEIN

B ob Stein is a graduate of Moody Bible Institute. He has degrees in psychology. His testimony was written in 1976.

My first real experience with the occult occurred at age nineteen. Until this time, I'd been a scientifically oriented person who dismissed the supernatural. I was somewhere between an agnostic and an atheist. Then, I purchased a book on witchcraft at a store in San Pedro. I practiced a candle–lighting ceremony according to the author's directions. I sensed some strange, eerie presence, became afraid, and never opened the book again.

At twenty–one, I moved to Berkeley, California to attend school. There, I became involved in various leftwing activities during my first year; food co–ops, Marxist study groups and anti–war activities. Yet something was missing from my life, something strange, mystical, and unknown. I was tired of my thoroughly analytical nature and majoring in computer science made me feel more and more lifeless, as if I had become a machine.

Many of the older radicals lived in my apartment building. Among these was an ex–SDS Weatherman named Stephen. Not only was Stephen heavily leftist, but also he practiced all sorts of occult–oriented activities. His Grandmother had taught him witchcraft, which he stated meant craft of the wise. From that point on, my life became more and more absorbed with occult–oriented activities. I frequently assisted Stephen during Tarot card reading and learned how to read cards myself.

In April of 1973, my roommates introduced me to the use of mescaline (a hallucinogenic drug). That evening, after visiting Stephen, I sat alone in my apartment reading a book on Tarot. The effects of the drug had significantly lessened as I began reading an Old Testament passage about the name for God (Jehovah), and how that name was the most powerful in heaven and earth. I felt a dark force enter the room, and, since I was Jewish, I called upon God to help me. I began weeping and said, "Oh, God, I'm just your child, let me serve You." I sensed God's presence in the room.

About three weeks later, I dropped out of school and received a very bazaar Tarot reading from Stephen, which did accurately predict disasters to follow. That summer, in order to avoid going home to Los Angeles, I worked for a small telephone company in Santa Rosa, California, laying cable. I began studying astrology in the nearby city of Sebastopol, and I started to do astrology charts and actively proclaim my beliefs to others.

Just prior to my return to Berkeley that fall, I had a gypsy read my cards. It was a typical forecast: "You will meet a girl, marry her, and she will be your only girl." The prophecy came to dominate my life and succeeded in chaining me more deeply to the occult. I vigilantly watched for the girl. I also began to augment my occult talents, becoming fascinated with the ancient Egyptians taking classes in Egyptology, and even attempting to learn hieroglyphics. My occult library grew, and I purchased more and more Tarot decks.

A girl attracted my attention, and the more I consulted Tarot, the more it assured me that she was the one. So, for two and one-half months I attempted to win the girl's heart, believing it impossible to fail. When, finally, she did begin to yield, the I Ching counseled me to retreat. The intervening six months were filled with anxiety for me. I felt as if I had gambled my entire life on the eventual success of this venture; but despite the apparent failure, I knew success would come eventually.

I continued to get more deeply involved in the occult. I compiled statistics for a research project on people's responses to Tarot readings, argued with the Psychology Department chairman that he should sponsor an occult symposium, and worked with the KFFA Premonitions Registry Bureau.

During this time, I became less able to distinguish reality from fantasy, and went through severe mood changes. I withdrew more and more into myself. Paranoid delusions gripped my personality as I fantasized myself getting the girl, only to lose her to my best friends. I insulted professors, created my own curriculum for classes, and finally dropped out of school.

I felt a deep revulsion for Christianity yet feared that I might turn to Christ. Stephen commended my anti-Christian feelings, since he practiced various forms of idolatry, worshipping the Celtic gods whom "His ancestors" worshiped. Because of my background, I felt drawn to worship the God of my fathers. I studied Kabballah and visited Chabad House, a Pharisaic Jewish organization. But still the issue remained unsettled in me.

Finally (after being drawn deeply into LSD and severely tempted to engage in homosexuality), I turned to Christ. After leaving Stephen's birthday party, I went to see some Christians. As I walked down University Avenue I felt literally pulled to go and talk to some astrologer friends, yet I didn't trust them. The Christian office was closed, and I began to become frantic. Then a car pulled up about five feet away and a Cuban preacher named Roberto got out. I came over to him and accepted Christ.

Deliverance has freed my personality. For the first time in my life, I'm learning who I really am. Before deliverance I was withdrawn and unable to communicate with people. Now I am much less self-conscious. I have a greater confidence in meeting the problems of life. I can express myself better. The demonic barrier, a sort of invisible wall that previously existed, has been torn down my Christ.

Prayer is now easier, as well, since I don't have to struggle with thoughts and emotions I previously experienced. I sense Christ's great love for me, and I no longer carry the burden of self-condemnation. I can now discern between the leading of God's Spirit, my old nature, and demonic leadings since going through deliverance.

When I pray, I no longer struggle against overcoming thoughts of blasphemy. The true peace and joy of Christ are now a daily reality. I now have complete assurance of my salvation. I have literally experienced the words of Scripture, "If the Son therefore shall make you free, ye shall be free indeed" (John 8:36).

APPENDIX 2

CHURCH FATHERS ON DELIVERANCE

The Fathers of the Early Church believed in and practiced deliverance. Here are quotes from three of the most famous Fathers on the subject:

JUSTIN MARTYR (c. 100–148 A.D.) Quoted from the Second Apology addressed to the Roman Senate:

> Numberless demoniacs throughout the whole world and in your city, many of our Christian men — casting them out in the name of Jesus Christ who was crucified under Pontius Pilate — have healed and do heal, rendering helpless and driving the possessing demons out of the men, though they could not be cured by any other exorcists, and those who use incantations and drugs.

CYPRIAN (c. 190–258 A.D.). After writing that demons inspire false prophets, and mix truth with falsehood to prove what they say, he added:

> Nevertheless, these evil spirits, commanded by the Living God immediately obey us, submit to us, own our power and are forced to come out of the bodies they possess.

TERTULLIAN (c. 160–230 A.D.). Quoted from his Apology addressed to the rulers of the Roman Empire:

> Let a person be brought before your tribunals who is plainly under demoniacal possession. The wicked spirit, bidden to speak by a follower of Christ, will as readily make the truthful confession that he is a demon, as elsewhere he has falsely asserted that he is a god. Or, if you will, let there be produced one of the god–possessed, as they are supposed — if they do not confess, in their fear of lying to a Christian, that they are demons, then there shed the blood of that most impudent follower of Christ. All the authority and power we have over them is from our naming the name of Christ, and recalling to their memory the woes with which God threatens them at the hand of Christ their judge, and which they expect one day to overtake them. Fearing Christ in God and God in Christ they become subject to the servants of God and Christ.

So at one touch and breathing, overwhelmed by the thought and realization of those judgment fires, they leave at our command the bodies they have entered, unwilling and distressed, and before your very eyes, put to an open shame.

APPENDIX 3

VALUABLE INSIGHTS FROM DEREK PRINCE

D erek Prince was engaged in deliverance ministry prior to when Don Basham began his work. Pastor Basham credits Pastor Prince with being a mentor.

In various places in this handbook, I related to some of Don Basham's insights and experiences. Here now I will relate some of what I learned from Derek Prince's book, *They Shall Expel Demons: What you Need to Know About Demons — Your Invisible Enemies.*

Derek Prince, in referring to Luke's account of Jesus' healing of a demon-possessed man (Luke 8:26–39), highlights a word found in verse 31: "abyss." Jesus had commanded the demons, "What is your name?" The response was, "Legion." And this legion of demons "begged him not to command them to depart into the abyss" (verse 31).

The Oxford Annotated Bible gives the following description of abyss: "a place of confinement for demonic forces, though hostile to God, are ultimately under his control." And then the following references are given: Revelation 9:1–11; 11:17; 17:8; 2-:1–3. Prince then states, "Jesus had a judicial authority."

Jesus had the authority to cast the demons into the abyss, otherwise known as the "pit of hell," and why He did not we do not understand. (As expressed elsewhere in this handbook, when I have also commanded demons to "go to the pit of hell," the demons strongly pleaded not to be sent there.)

Prince, as well as Basham, asked demons to name themselves. Having learned from them, during the 1970s and on, I did the same, not always but occasionally. We know it has biblical support, since Jesus did this in the story of the Legion in Luke 8. It is thought that knowing a demon's name helps in the deliverance. "Fear" was a name demons sometimes gave, so we would probe to find the dynamics of this and help a person recover from various fears. Or "hate" would be the demon's answer. Then this led to finding out who was hated or what was hated, and forgiveness sought — healing was the goal.

Despite this, the question remains: will demons tell the truth? We know that Satan is a liar and the father of lies (see John 8:44). At this point, I am not fully confident that asking a demon to name itself is proper.

Here are the steps Prince counsels in a group deliverance situation (p. 64):

He lays out four simple conditions that must be met by those in the group:

1. Be sure you have repented — that is, turned away from every form of sin.
2. Look only to Jesus; He alone is the Deliverer.
3. Base your appeal solely on what Jesus did for you through His death on the cross, not on any "good works" of your own.
4. Be sure that, by an act of your will, you have forgiven every person who ever harmed or wronged you.

With that, he then instructs the group that, "In the name of Jesus you have the authority to expel them from yourselves" (p. 64).

Prince repeatedly emphasizes the barriers to deliverance: failure to repent and the failure to forgive others and surrender resentment against them.

Those who do deliverance ministry are often criticized for doing this work. One reason is that Satan carefully guards the secrets of the demonic kingdom and does not want them discovered. "Over the centuries he has built up in the minds of Christians a barrier of fear and superstitious ignorance keeping us from acknowledging either the truths of Scripture or the facts of experience" (p. 68).

A second reason is that the church has established what is proper and appropriate for "the house of God." Dignity holds sway, and deliverance ministry is not a dignified ministry. He then describes what a mess deliverance ministry can be:

> I looked again at the ministry of Jesus and discovered various instances in which a demon or demons screamed and shouted at Him, interrupted His preaching, convulsed people when they came out, leaving them apparently dead; caused a person to wallow on the ground foaming at the mouth; and stampeded a herd of two thousand pigs into a lake. Yet Jesus was never disturbed, nor did He suppress these manifestations. He simply dealt with them as part of His total ministry to suffering humanity. (p. 68)

Because of the importance Prince assigns to Revelation chapter 12, I will present it here without comment. The interpretation of various subjects in the chapter are open to debate, still those doing the messy work will benefit from the passage:

REVELATION 12:

The Woman and the Dragon

[1] And a great sign appeared in heaven: a woman clothed with the sun, with the moon under her feet, and on her head a crown of twelve stars. [2] She was pregnant and was crying out in birth pains and the agony of giving birth. [3] And another sign appeared in heaven: behold, a great red dragon, with seven heads and ten horns, and on his heads seven diadems. [4] His tail swept down a third of the stars of heaven and cast them to the earth. And the dragon stood before the woman who was about to give birth, so that when she bore her child he might devour it. [5] She gave birth to a male child, one who is to rule all the nations with a rod of iron, but her child was caught up to God and to his throne, [6] and the woman fled into the wilderness, where she has a place prepared by God, in which she is to be nourished for 1,260 days.

Satan Thrown Down to Earth

[7] Now war arose in heaven, Michael and his angels fighting against the dragon. And the dragon and his angels fought back, [8] but he was defeated, and there was no longer any place for them in heaven. [9] And the great dragon was thrown down, that ancient serpent, who is called the devil and Satan, the deceiver of the whole world—he was thrown down to the earth, and his angels were thrown down with him. [10] And I heard a loud voice in heaven, saying, "Now the salvation and the power and the kingdom of our God and the authority of his Christ have come, for the accuser of our brothers has been thrown down, who accuses them day and night before our God. [11] And they have conquered him by the blood of the Lamb and by the word of their testimony, for they loved not their lives even unto death. [12] Therefore, rejoice, O heavens and you who dwell in them! But woe to you, O earth and sea, for the devil has come down to you in great wrath, because he knows that his time is short!"

[13] And when the dragon saw that he had been thrown down to the earth, he pursued the woman who had given birth to the male child. [14] But the woman was given the two wings of the great eagle so that she might fly from the serpent into the wilderness, to the place where she is to be nourished for a time, and times, and half a time. [15] The serpent poured water like a river out of his mouth after the woman, to sweep her away with a flood. [16] But the earth came to the help of the woman, and the earth opened its mouth and swallowed the river that the dragon had poured from his mouth. [17] Then the dragon became furious with the woman and went off to make war on the rest of her

offspring, on those who keep the commandments of God and hold to the testimony of Jesus. And he stood on the sand of the sea. (ESV)

Prince cites a false claim often made: "Demons will leave me alone if I leave them alone." I agree with Prince here. Nothing could be further from the truth. In fact, we have little idea how much, how often, and in what ways the demonic kingdom intrudes into our world. We barely catch glimpses.

Demons mimic human beings: they have will, emotions, intellect, self-awareness, and the ability to communicate via speech (pp. 89-90).

The origin of demons is mentioned in Scripture. Generally, two ideas are put forth. One, demons are angels who followed Day Star, son of Dawn, otherwise known as Lucifer, in a heavenly rebellion (see Isaiah 14:15). Two, they are spirits of a pre-Adamic race, an idea which is not presented in Scripture. (I lean strongly to the first, but I thought it important to present the other view.)

Though he worked in the Pentecostal/charismatic wing of Christianity, Prince does bring a critique of the misuse of prophecy in some circles, which he describes as being nothing less than fortunetelling. I heartedly agree on this point, especially since I experienced and participated, to some extent, in this kind of proceeding during the 1970s. Unhappily, this tendency is not only continuing but is being encouraged, especially in churches aligned with the New Apostolic Reformation.

Prince points out that the Greek word translated "sorcery" in Revelation 9:20–21 means drugs. The Greek word here is transliterated *pharmakeion*, and we get the word "pharmacy" from it. I believe Prince is saying that the use of drugs, substances that induce the passive or altered state of consciousness, are a gateway to demonization. My own work corroborates this.

He moves on then to delineate dangerous spiritualities (p. 122 and following):

1. One, the teaching of a plurality of gods, and he references 1 Corinthians 8:5–6.
2. Two, idol worship — Exodus 20:3–5.
3. Three, the idea that human beings can become gods — Genesis 3:5.
4. Four, having access to special knowledge and power — 1 Timothy 6:20–21.
5. Five, the process of initiation and secret rites.

A key verse for Prince here is 1 Corinthians 10:20: "I imply that what pagans sacrifice they offer to demons and not to God. I do not want you to be participants with demons."

Always one of the main issues during the era when Don Basham and Derek Prince conducted deliverance ministry was whether or not Christians could be indwelt by a demon. Here Prince goes to 1 Peter 5:8–9:

> Be sober minded, be watchful. Your adversary the devil prowls around like a roaring lion, seeking someone to devour. Resist him, firm in your faith, knowning that the same kinds of suffering are being experienced by your brotherhood throughout the world.

Peter clearly addresses this passage to Christians. Two other passages along this line are 2 Corinthians 11:3–4 and 1 Timothy 4:1.

On page 165, Prince describes the purpose of demons. One, to torment and afflict people. Two, prevent a person from coming to Christ. Failing that, three, to keep the Christian from serving Christ well.

Prince counsels those preparing for deliverance to enter into the victory Jesus has won for us (see 1 Corinthians 15:57) and look for someone to minister deliverance or go to Jesus yourself and ask Him to cast out the demons.

He reminds his readers that demons often come out with crying, screaming, roaring, spitting, or vomiting, therefore have tissues and towels on hand. And, lastly, we do not shout at demons; a firm voice will do.

VALUABLE INSIGHTS FROM RICHARD GALLAGHER

I was stunned by Dr. Richard Gallagher's book, *Demonic Foes*. A Roman Catholic psychiatrist who has been involved in countless exorcisms, working with Catholic exorcists and others, Gallagher has helped frequently with evaluations prior to the actual Rite of Major Exorcism. I recommend his book to all who consider engaging in deliverance ministry and consider it a must read. It was published October 6, 2020, and I had three copies by October 8th.

During the 1970s, due to my book, published by Zondervan Publishing House in 1973, I was contacted by the San Francisco Archdiocese's exorcist, because he had read the manual. After meeting and discussing the circumstances of various cases, he started calling me in to assist in exorcisms. I do not recall his name now, but he was a retired priest, a tall, gray haired, and a very humble and pleasant man. We experienced some rather wild deliverances. At first, I assisted in the Rite of Major Exorcism, such as it was in that day, but after a while we started doing deliverance in my more direct style. After some years, he dropped out of sight. No more phone calls, so I can only assume he died. I will never forget those days.

This simple account may help you understand why I so welcomed Dr. Gallagher's book. From here on I will identify Dr. Gallagher by his initials, RG or by Doctor.

RG asks, "Do the patient's symptoms have a natural or scientific explanation?" (p. 8). The answer can be illusive. For many, "possessions may be thought to fall into the psychiatric categories of various psychoses and severe personality and dissociative disorders, or they may seem to happen to individuals who are prone to suggestibility." And the Doctor looks at these issues carefully when called in to make an analysis.

In an attempt to solve the riddle, physical exams are used along with all the standard medical tests, blood work, brain scans, EEG, and more. Then a "narrative assessment" is made along with a symptom survey. In addition, family members and friends are interviewed to confirm, or not, what the patient has reported.

RG uses three terms to describe how the demonic may impact a person/patient. One is possession, then oppression, and finally, infestation. The most serious is possession, meaning a person is under the "control" of demons. Oppression is less serious, but demons are crushing down on a person and may be attacking physically where scratches and bruises are left. Then infestation, where demonic or paranormal events are evident in the person's environment.

On page 11, RG says, "the Rite of Major Exorcism is not a magic formula that will cast out demons automatically and completely liberate suffering victims without effort from the afflicted individuals themselves." "Magic formula" in my mind includes the use of Holy Water and other "blessed objects" such as a priest's stole, so RG left me wondering here and reminded me of the 1970s work with the Catholic exorcist. Yet in various parts of the book, RG does not promote the use of magic formulas.

Here now is an important quote found on pages 33 and 34:

> Possessions and oppressions can, in my view, be consistently distin-
> guished from both mental and physical disorders by an expert. But one
> needs a lot of experience. It is especially important that spiritual advis-
> ers, who often know little about psychiatric or medical disorders, work
> closely with mental health or medical professions when dealing with
> oppressive situations. It helps to have a thorough knowledge of both
> medical/psychiatric illnesses and typically oppressive features as well
> as an appreciation of the likely causes.

I give this lengthy quote, since most of us who have a calling to this ministry cannot come anywhere close to the expertise RG is speaking of. Deliverance is a mystery, according to my diagnosis. And yet I appreciate this careful approach to the matter and would be inclined to utilize such, if it were possible.

Reading through *Demonic Foes* I found little mention of Jesus, the Bible, the cross, repentance, forgiveness, and so on—words and phrases liberally distributed in other books on deliverance, until I reached the book's ending. Here, RG began to speak in what one might call "evangelical" terminology. I decided not to make too much of the absence of such in the early parts of the book.

The Doctor presents the case of one "Julia," a member of a Satanic cult, a high priestess who realized she was in trouble of sorts and approached the Catholic Church for help. Here now is what he wrote following a consultation with her in his office:

> During the exorcisms of most full possessions, the evil spirit may on

its own (or may be forced to) manifest itself and display its remark-able preternatural powers. Even outside the exorcism, and critical to the diagnostic process, victims in their periodic possessed trances fre-quently display at least some of the classic signs of their state. Evil spir-its may speak foreign languages; show supernormal strength; or reveal "hidden knowledge," that is, display an awareness of matters they have no natural way of knowing—akin to what psychics claim to be able to do. Of course, it is the demon who has such powers, not the victim. In a possession, the demonstration of these paranormal abilities is precisely what proves that a foreign evil spirit is present and in control. Despite occasional protestations by the so-called parapsychologists and spiri-tualists, human beings on their own have none of these powers (p. 45).

The Doctor also says, on the same page 45, of those who commit to worshiping Satan, that "Satan grants his devotees the ability to demonstrate psychic powers not only outside an overt possessed state, but also in their normal conscious state."

This is my own experience as well. In other words, Satan rewards his follow-ers with favors. And this is always, and I mean always, the draw. Some forms of power, extra ordinary knowledge, satisfaction of lustful desires, means to punish enemies, even acquisition of wealth—yes, Satan is a giver of gifts, at least at first. Then things change, and the punishing torments begin.

Julia, the high priestess of Satan, derided those who followed traditional reli-gion, saying they are unnatural and repressed. "'My philosophy is this, doc.' She told me. 'Indulgence instead of abstinence. Vital existence instead of spiritual pipe dreams. Vengeance instead of turning the other cheek'" (p. 46).

Another note from my own experience: the "indulgence" has to do with sex and seems to satisfy early on but turns into just sex, then moves to bad sex. Julia became a "breeder" whose pregnancies supplied aborted fetuses for satanic rit-uals. Hardly satisfying!

RG is a psychiatrist, and on page 47 he made a statement I would like to put up in large neon letters for all who do deliverance ministry to read: "If you say little, people often tell you everything." As a counselor and a pastor, this rings so very true and is particularly relevant in dealing with those who need deliverance. They may so very much want to keep quiet about some of the more awful expe-riences, especially around sexuality, and it can get ugly.

A story now.

I think it was in 1969, and I was heading out the door to continue a painting job I had in Kentfield, Marin County. There on the porch was a teenaged girl. I said hello, can I help you? but she was mute. My wife came to the door to see what was going on, so I turned to her and asked if she would take care of this little person, as I had to get on with it. She looked at me, shook her head, and retreated back into the house. Only one thing to do, so I took her with me to the job.

In was an interior job, and I set about tarping the front room. I sat the girl in a chair in front of a fireplace. She still had not uttered a word. After a few hours, I was busy cutting in along a wall and the ceiling. Across the room, directly opposite me, sat the girl. With paint brush in hand, standing on a step ladder, something abruptly came to my consciousness. I shuddered inwardly, put the brush in the paint can and turned to her. Right off, without explanation or anything else I said, "I know what happened to you. You were being initiated into a satanic cult last night and after wild, weird sex you were commanded to lick the cum out of the female sheep the male initiates had just had sex with." (I had never before heard of such a thing.)

She began to wildly sob and sob and sob. As quickly as I could, I finished up the living room, packed up, and headed home with her in tow. I elicited the family phone number from her and made the call. The next day, the parents flew in, came to our home, and within minutes were out the door with her.

I have wondered all these years if this poor runaway had received any deliverance.

When RG asked why Julia had been drawn to satanism, she replied: "It's because we get a lot in return. We worship Satan because he looks after us and grants us big favors." And oddly, one of these favors is "remote viewing," which she demonstrated to the Doctor early on, describing to him what he had been doing the previous evening. In Satan she found pleasure and power.

My own experience has shown me that Satanic rites are designed to produce guilt and shame in the participants, allowing the priests and priestesses to assert that once the acts are carried out, there is no forgiveness from God, so you might as well serve the devil all out. Have no illusions—this is really how it works.

RG writes that possession and oppression exist on a continuum; they can be minor or all the way to severe in their impact upon a person—sometimes light, other times heavy. But "the essence of possession is the actual control of the body (never the "soul" or will) of a person by one or more evil spirits. At its full manifestation, victims are no longer acting on their own accord; the demon has taken charge of their functioning, and periodically at least, their consciousness" (p. 80). A spirit may be controlling, then seem to disappear, but it does not leave the body. They can seem to come and go, even rather quickly.

When under fairly full control of a person, a demon may begin to speak and will use "vile and blasphemous language with a decided arrogance" (p. 81). I, too, have seen this often, and it rather easy to see the difference. While the demon is staring straight at you, the victim seems not to be at home.

RG describes "signs," though they may vary greatly, which may be seen in the worst cases. The official manual for exorcists lists three signs: the ability to speak an unknown language, the awareness of hidden knowledge, and various abnormal physical signs, especially immense strength, but also humanly impossible bodily 'movements,' extreme contortions, and even the rare levitation" (p. 81).

An observation: "Invite the devil in, and he will try to take over the house" (p. 86).

The Doctor takes special note of James 4:7. He knows the power and necessity of resisting the devil.

Demons will attempt to present themselves, that is internally to those they indwell, as dead souls, angels, or a deity of a pagan religion. This is an observation of RG's widely known among those who do deliverance ministry. A persona of a dead soul, an angel, Zeus, Jupiter, etc. will often be dropped as the demon reveals who it really is, a demon.

My observations, and those also of RG, are that when people turn to occult practices or otherwise attract demons, they will eventually want to be free of the demonic turmoil, and that is when the demons begin to seriously act out. It is at this point that the phone rings or an email or text is received from someone who needs deliverance ministry.

Another point I want to weigh in on here: RG uses the terms possession, oppression, and infestation; however, these distinctions are not found in Scripture. Rather we find only demonization or demonized, so there are really no shades or different conditions of the demonic presence in my view. That said, the three terms may well describe what is observed in a demonized person; it is not a cookie-cutter situation.

An important point on an issue, one that has consistently confused me is, "To state the obvious again, physical and psychological impairments are different from spiritual ailments instigated by demons. Medically ill patients do not suffer paranormal features and rarely have in their backgrounds the kind of factors that lead to such attacks" (p. 114). To this I can agree, but to someone as uneducated as I am in these matters, to grasp the difference is somewhat elusive.

Then again, RG admits that there can be a combination of medical and demonic disorders in an afflicted person. What to do with this? I hope you are not expecting an answer from me. I am saying this, because I want to make it clear that in deliverance ministry, everything is not clear and clean.

I am going to insert a rather lengthy passage, found on page 129, that some readers may find helpful:

> Speaking of the ideal exorcist, the Roman Ritual calls for someone not only "outstanding in knowledge" but also with personal qualities such as maturity and holiness. Overly emotional or poorly educated ministers or priests, just like ill-informed doctors or lawyers, don't make good judges of complex situations, such as demonic states, that require patience, caution, and sober judgment. Some astute and experienced exorcists are knowledgeable enough to discern diabolic attacks largely on their own. Still, they are advised to seek a medical professional's opinion whenever any doubt or other medical needs arise—a sacred role passed down in my profession for centuries.

The Doctor does not think much of the book, *Pigs in the Parlor: A Practical Guide to Deliverance*, which I was happy to see, as I did not think much of it in earlier days either. That book caused me personally a great deal of grief, as it turned much about everyone's life into something dark, spooky, and demonic. A real case of casting the net too broadly.

RG writes: "Catholic prayers or exorcism are classified as either 'deprecatory,' asking for God's help, or 'imprecatory,' commanding the devil to leave. Though the formal rite combines both, only ordained priests can recite imprecatory prayers." Of course, the means I employ, and also most other non-Catholics, focus on the "imprecatory" commanding demons to come out.

In the Rite of Major Exorcism, it is common that the exorcist asks the demon for its name and then asks it when it will leave. Also, the exorcist will command the demon to leave. This is not much different from many deliverance sessions I have either conducted or witnessed. Most exorcists prefer conducting deliverance sessions in a church setting, "often in a room where the Eucharist is present" (p. 144), though that has not been a rule I have followed.

The Doctor speaks at the close of his book about the sensationalizing of exorcisms, with stories of these gone wrong. These I have witnessed myself and is one of the reasons I have hoped to never again get involved with it all. RG writes, "The argument among critics of exorcism is that such abuses justify doing away with exorcisms altogether" (p. 234).

With this I can identify. While most deliverance sessions are clean, things can go sideways, and in the world today this can be very dangerous. I must say that I am not at all certain that the signing of a waver would avail much. Yet, this is the world we live in, and we cannot be intimidated by the confusion evil spirits create. We must be as careful as we possibly can, especially when bringing into this ministry only those who are really up to it.

I will end now with some remarks RG makes as he closes out his book. All of these are on pages 242 and 243:

> My own experience and the collective wisdom of centuries suggest that demons are indeed dedicated to destroying human beings—preferably spiritually, but also physically. The whole business seems odd.... Why, I am often asked, would evil spirits choose to assault and even to take over a person's body?

> "Sadism and misery love company," I'm sure are parts of the answer. But further, the deeper, time-honored explanation involves the idea of their despising humans because of their ultimate envy and hatred of God.... And, it also seems, their loathsome activity is directed to the image of the divine reflected in all of us human creatures. Yes, they want to corrupt us and win us to their "side."

> The demonic world seeks to negate our loving personalities, destroy us spiritually, and, if it can, even cause our physical death.

> One philosopher opined that Satan and evil spirits would kill us all if not prevented. I used to think this view a sort of superstitious, medieval hyperbole. But now I believe it is a statement of fact.

Thanks to Dr. Richard Gallagher for this most helpful book.

Recommended Books

Here is a short list of books that might be consulted to prepare one for deliverance ministry. There are hundreds of books on the subject with new ones appearing regularly.

Basham, Don, *Deliver Us from Evil: A Pastor's Reluctant Encounters with the Powers of Darkness*. Minneapolis, Minnesota: Chosen Books, 1972.

Beverly, Stanley. *The Body of Christ's Need for Bible-Based Deliverance Ministry*. Maitland, FL: Xulon Press, 2020.

Gallagher, Richard. *Demonic Foes: My Twenty-five Years as a Psychiatrist Investigating Possessions, Diabolic Attacks, and the Paranormal*. Harper One, 2020.

Gondwe, Eric. *Major Spiritual Warfare and Deliverance Ministry Principles*. Jesusw.com and Spiritualwarfaredeliverance.co, 2006.

Guiley, Rosemary Ellen. *The Encyclopedia of Demons and Demonology*, Checkmark Books, 2009.

Horrobin, Peter. *Healing through Deliverance, vol. 2: The Practice of Deliverance Ministry*. Chosen Books, 2003.

Moody, Gene M. *The Complete Deliverance Manual*. Createspace Independent Publishing Platform, 2016.

Philpott, Kent. *Deliver Us from Evil: How Jesus Casts Out Demons Today*. San Rafael, California: Earthen Vessel Media, 2014.

_____. The Soul Journey: How Shamanism, Santeria, Wicca, and Charisma are Connected. San Rafael, California. Earthen Vessel Media, 2014.

_____. *A Manual of Demonology and the Occult*. San Rafael, California. Earthen Vessel Media, 2021.

_____. *The Ouija Board*. San Rafael, California. Earthen Vessel Media, 2020.

Prince, Derek, *They Shall Expel Demons*. Grand Rapids, Michigan: Chosen Books, 1999.

Unger, Merrill F. *Biblical Demonology: A Study of Spiritual Forces Today*. Kregel Publications, 2011.

CPSIA information can be obtained
at www.ICGtesting.com
Printed in the USA
BVHW070111140421
604815BV00008B/565